THE SUCCESSION NARRATIVE

STUDIES IN BIBLICAL THEOLOGY

A series of monographs designed to provide clergy and laymen with the best
work in biblical scholarship both in this country and abroad

Advisory Editors:

C. F. D. MOULE, *Lady Margaret's Professor of Divinity in the University of Cambridge*

JAMES BARR, *Professor of Semitic Languages and Literatures,
University of Manchester*

PETER ACKROYD, *Samuel Davidson Professor of Old Testament Studies,
University of London*

FLOYD V. FILSON, *Professor of New Testament Literature and History,
McCormick Theological Seminary, Chicago*

G. ERNEST WRIGHT, *Professor of Old Testament History and Theology
at Harvard University*

STUDIES IN BIBLICAL THEOLOGY

Second Series . 9

THE SUCCESSION NARRATIVE

A Study of II Samuel 9-20; I Kings 1 and 2

R. N. WHYBRAY

SCM PRESS LTD
BLOOMSBURY STREET LONDON

SBN 334 01535 9
© SCM PRESS LTD 1968
FIRST PUBLISHED 1968
PRINTED IN GREAT BRITAIN BY
ROBERT CUNNINGHAM AND SONS LTD
ALVA

To
The Very Reverend
Dr C. A. Simpson
Dean of Christ Church, Oxford
who first aroused my interest
in the Succession Narrative

ACKNOWLEDGMENT

I here record my appreciation of the help given to me by my friend and colleague, Mrs Mary Tanner, who read the typescript most carefully and made a number of criticisms from which the book in its final form has benefited.

CONTENTS

Abbreviations   ix

I INTRODUCTION   1

II THE CHARACTER AND PURPOSE OF THE SUCCESSION
   NARRATIVE   10
   1 The Succession Narrative as history   11
   2 The Succession Narrative as a novel   19
      a. Unity of theme   19
      b. Structure   25
      c. Use of dialogue   34
      d. Portrayal of character   35
      e. Style   45
   3 The Succession Narrative as a national epic   47
   4 The Succession Narrative as a moral or religious tale   49
   5 The Succession Narrative as political propaganda   50

III WISDOM IN THE SUCCESSION NARRATIVE   56
    A. THE SUCCESSION NARRATIVE AND THE BOOK OF
       PROVERBS: A GENERAL COMPARISON   56
    1 The importance of 'counsel'   57
    2 Retribution   60
    3 Yahweh as the controller of human destiny   62
    4 Attitude towards the cult   66
    5 Conclusion   71

    B. THE SUCCESSION NARRATIVE AS DIDACTIC LITERATURE   71
    1 The use of narrative in wisdom literature   72
    2 The Joseph Narrative and the Succession Narrative   76
    3 The Succession Narrative as a dramatization of
       proverbial wisdom   78

vii

IV THE POLITICAL NOVEL IN EGYPT AND ISRAEL 96

1 The 'royal novel' in Egypt 98
2 The 'royal novel' in the Old Testament 100
3 The Egyptian novel and the Succession Narrative 101
4 Political aspects of Egyptian and Israelite literature 105
5 The Succession Narrative and the *Instruction of Amenemhet* 110
6 Conclusion 115

Index of Authors 117

ABBREVIATIONS

ANET	*Ancient Near Eastern Texts Relating to the Old Testament*, ed. by J. B. Pritchard, Princeton, 1950; 2nd ed., 1955
BWANT	Beiträge zur Wissenschaft vom Alten und Neuen Testament
HAT	Handbuch zum Alten Testament, ed. by O. Eissfeldt, Tübingen
HTR	*Harvard Theological Review*
ICC	The International Critical Commentary, ed. by S. R. Driver, A. Plummer and C. A. Briggs, Edinburgh
JBL	*Journal of Biblical Literature*
JEA	*Journal of Egyptian Archaeology*
OTL	The Old Testament Library, London and Philadelphia
RB	*Revue Biblique*
RHPR	*Revue d'Histoire et de Philosophie religieuses*
SBT	Studies in Biblical Theology, London
TC	Torch Bible Commentaries, London
TLZ	*Theologische Literaturzeitung*
VT	*Vetus Testamentum*
VT Suppl.	Supplements to *Vetus Testamentum*
ZAW	*Zeitschrift für die alttestamentliche Wissenschaft*

I

INTRODUCTION

RECENT study has demonstrated that the early monarchy in Israel was a period of exceptional intellectual and cultural advance.[1] This was a natural concomitant of the material achievements of David: the establishment for the first time of a strong Israelite state led to a new national consciousness, a greatly increased economic prosperity and the development of a new, relatively leisured class with wider interests and more extensive international contacts than had ever before been known in Israel.[2] The biblical tradition concerning Solomon's intellectual and cultural activities (I Kings 4.29-34; I Kings 5.9-14 in the Hebrew) has often been interpreted as evidence that this 'cultural enlightenment' began with him; but whatever Solomon's contribution may have been, it was the reign of David which marked the real break with earlier traditions, and we ought probably to think of David as the real innovator in this as in so many other spheres of activity.

One of the main causes of this 'enlightenment' was that Israel was now brought for the first time into full and continuous contact with that intellectual tradition, common to all the civilized peoples of the ancient near East, which we know as wisdom. This tradition was not entirely unfamiliar to the Israelites: their Mesopotamian origins, sojourn in Egypt and relations with Canaanite cities both before and after the settlement in Canaan

---

[1] See *inter alia* A. Alt, 'Die Weisheit Salomos', *TLZ* 76, 1951, cols. 139-144=*Kleine Schriften* II, Munich, 1953, pp. 90-99; O. Eissfeldt, 'Religionshistorie und Religionspolemik im alten Testament', VT Suppl. 3, 1955, pp. 94-102; K. Galling, *Die Krise der Aufklärung in Israel* (Mainzer Universitäts-Reden 19), Mainz, 1952; G. von Rad, *Old Testament Theology* I, Edinburgh, 1962, pp. 49ff.; E. Würthwein, *Die Weisheit Ägyptens und das alte Testament*, Marburg, 1960.

[2] On this class see especially H. Duesberg, *Les scribes inspirés*, 2nd edn, Maredsous, 1966, pp. 99-176.

[3] Here I agree with J. L. McKenzie's recent 'Reflections on Wisdom', *JBL* 86, 1967, pp. 1-9. Cf. also R. B. Y. Scott, *Proverbs and Ecclesiastes* (Anchor Bible), New York, 1965, pp. xxxff.

I

had undoubtedly given them some knowledge of it,[4] and this is reflected in some of the earliest Old Testament texts[5]; but it was only from the time of David, when the Canaanite cities came under Israelite control, and official contacts were established with the neighbouring states, that it made its full impact.

It was mediated principally through a new class of officials or scribes, which David was obliged to establish to assist him in the task of organizing and governing the large and complex empire which had so unexpectedly fallen into his hands. Israel was now a major power, and was inevitably drawn into the world of international politics. It was essential that it should have a ruling class no less efficient than those of the neighbouring states, capable not only of governing the empire but also of participating on equal terms in international diplomacy, which in the ancient near East at that time was an indispensable function of state, conducted with considerable finesse.[6] It was also necessary, for reasons of prestige, that the royal court should be brilliant and impressive, and in no way inferior to foreign courts. The grandiloquent descriptions of Solomon's court in I Kings 4ff. show the importance which was attached to this.

For such an undertaking, foreign assistance was indispensable: the Israelites had no previous experience of such matters. David was no doubt able to rely to some extent on the help of the officials of Jerusalem and the other former Canaanite city-states who had become his subjects. These states had for a long period been in a state of vassalage to Egypt, and had no doubt retained much of the Egyptian administrative machinery during the interval which had followed the Egyptian withdrawal.[7] In Jerusalem itself, David would have found such a class of officials ready to hand when he took it and made it his capital. But these officials

---

[4] See H. Cazelles, 'Les débuts de la sagesse en Israël' in *Les sagesses du proche orient ancien* (Bibliothèque des centres d'études supérieurs spécialisés), Paris, 1963, pp. 27-40.

[5] E.g. the 'wise ladies' in Judg. 5.29; the parable of Jotham, Judg. 9.8ff.

[6] N. K. Gottwald, *All the Kingdoms of the Earth*, New York, 1964, pp. 30-46.

[7] The Amarna Letters give some idea of the extent of Egyptian influence on the Canaanite cities. For a selection of these letters with explanatory notes see *ANET*, pp. 483-490 (annotated by W. F. Albright), and D. Winton Thomas, *Documents from Old Testament Times*, London, 1958, pp. 38-45 (annotated by C. J. Mullo Weir).

will have been too few for his needs, and their experience hardly adequate for his purposes.

There is evidence that he sought and obtained direct assistance from foreign powers. The contemporary lists of ministers of state during his reign and that of Solomon (II Sam. 8.16-18; 20.23-26; I Kings 4.2-6) include the titles of offices which are translations of foreign, especially Egyptian, titles: the *mazkīr* or herald, the *sōpēr* or secretary and the (*ʾašer*) *ʿal-habbayit* or governor of the royal household. To these may be added that of the 'king's friend' which appears in II Sam. 15.37; 16.16 in the form *rēʿe dāwīd*, 'David's friend'.[8] The foreign names which appear in these lists[9] show that some of these offices were filled by foreigners, whom David employed in civilian posts as he also employed them in military ones.[10] It is probable that court ceremonial, especially the coronation and enthronement, was also devised partly in imitation of foreign models.[11]

For the training of a permanent body of Israelite scribes there must necessarily have been established at Jerusalem a school or schools similar to those which existed in Egypt and Babylonia[12]; and at first the teachers must have been foreign scribes whose instruction, though no doubt adapted for Israelite needs, was derived from foreign sources. This dependence on a foreign educational tradition has been proved by recent study of the Book of Proverbs: this book is now seen to consist for the most part of a series of school textbooks whose contents correspond closely to Egyptian—and to some extent Mesopotamian—works of the same type,[13] and there are now grounds for believing that much

---

[8] R. de Vaux, 'Titres et fonctionnaires égyptiens à la cour de David et de Salomon', *RB* 48, 1939, pp. 394-405 and *Ancient Israel. Its Life and Institutions*, London, 1961, pp. 127-132; J. Begrich, 'Sôfēr und Mazkīr', *ZAW* 58, 1940, pp. 1-29; H. Donner, 'Der "Freund des Königs"', *ZAW* 73, 1961, pp. 269-277; M. Noth, *Könige* (Biblischer Kommentar), Neukirchen, 1963, pp. 63ff.

[9] Adoram, Abda, Shisha (and its variant Shavsha in I Chron. 18.16), Elihoreph.

[10] Uriah the Hittite, the Cherethites and Pelethites, and Ittai the Gittite.

[11] G. von Rad, 'The Royal Ritual in Judah', *The Problem of the Hexateuch and Other Essays*, Edinburgh, 1966, pp. 222-231; translated from *TLZ* 72, 1947, cols. 211-216.

[12] On Egyptian and Babylonian education see H. Brunner, *Altägyptische Erziehung*, Wiesbaden, 1957; G. R. Driver, *Semitic Writing* (Schweich Lectures, 1944), London, 1948, pp. 62ff.; L. Dürr, *Das Erziehungswesen im alten Testament und im antiken Orient*, Leipzig, 1932.

[13] E.g. H. Gressmann, *Israels Spruchweisheit im Zusammenhang der Welt-*

of its teaching was available in Israel before the death of David.[14] It was through these scribal schools that the international wisdom tradition made its chief impact on Israel. The education which they imparted was liberal rather than merely vocational: training in administration and diplomacy was regarded as inseparable from the wider aspects of human life and experience. The scribes were an intellectual as well as a political elite, and their education, as the wisdom literature shows, inculcated a distinctive attitude towards man and the world.

Among its characteristics was a pragmatic and rational outlook. The wisdom of the scribes was an activity pursued independently of religious institutions, which exhibited a detached curiosity about the natural world and about human nature. Recent studies have shown the influence on the Old Testament of this spirit of enquiry in such fields as natural history and geography.[15]

The new spirit thus introduced into Israel's ruling circles could not fail to have a profound effect upon traditional religious beliefs. 'The early monarchical period saw a wholly new departure in spirituality, a kind of "enlightenment", an awakening of spiritual self-consciousness. Men became aware of their own spiritual and rational powers, and whole dimensions of experience opened up before their eyes, inwardly as well as outwardly. They were dimensions of which the faith of their forefathers had taken no account.'[16]

The new vision of man inevitably affected the understanding of God's relation to man and therefore of Yahweh's particular

---

literatur, Berlin, 1925; P. Humbert, *Recherches sur les sources égyptiennes de la littérature sapientiale d'Israël*, Neuchâtel, 1929; B. Gemser, *Sprüche* (HAT), 1937, 2nd edn, 1963; R. N. Whybray, *Wisdom in Proverbs* (SBT 45), London, 1965; Duesberg, *op. cit.*

[14] For justification of this statement see pp. 78ff. *infra*. Cf. McKenzie, *art. cit.*, p. 5. The only parts of Proverbs which are necessarily later than the early monarchy are some passages in chs. 1-9 (Whybray, *op. cit.*). Even this reservation has been challenged by C. Kayatz, who in *Studien zu Proverbien 1-9*, Neukirchen, 1966 maintains that these passages also are from the time of Solomon.

[15] See especially the articles of Alt, Eissfeldt and Galling cited above, p. 1, n. 1, and M. Noth, 'Die Bewährung von Salomos "Göttlicher Weisheit"', VT Suppl. 3, 1955, pp. 225-237.

[16] G. von Rad, 'The Joseph Narrative and Ancient Wisdom', (*Problem of the Hexateuch*, pp. 292-300; translated from VT Suppl. 1, 1953, pp. 120-127), p. 293.

relationship with Israel. Not that the new influences of thought were purely secular: they did not deny God's relationship with man, but they conceived of it in a new way. 'Now for the first time it was possible to understand God's activity in an all-embracing sense. It is no longer seen as something which operates from time to time through the charisma of a chosen leader, but as a much more constant, much more widely embracing factor concealed in the whole breadth of secular affairs, and pervading every single sphere of human life.'[17]

These new ideas naturally expressed themselves in literature. In the Book of Proverbs we find a type of literature which is concerned wholly with individual man and his welfare, and expresses the newly acquired ideas about human nature and its possibilities, though at the same time it asserts man's ultimate subordination to the principle of just retribution, which is identified with the righteous will of Yahweh as ruler of the world.

In recent years it has been shown that the concepts which dominated the wisdom literature proper were not without influence on other literary genres. Such influence is to be found, for example, in the prophetical books,[18] in Deuteronomy,[19] and perhaps even in the Decalogue.[20] This is not unexpected, since in Egypt also wisdom had a wide influence on literature generally.[21]

It is not to be supposed that the Israelite reaction to the invasion of the wisdom tradition was entirely passive. The Book of Proverbs, though deeply influenced by foreign wisdom, is nevertheless an Israelite composition in which this has been adapted for Israelite needs. Even more significantly, the Israelites seem to have begun early to make their own experiments with the literary possibilities of wisdom. It has been suggested by Alt[22] and Noth[23] that the statement in I Kings 4.32f. (Heb. 5.12f.)

[17] G. von Rad, 'The Beginnings of Historical Writing in Ancient Israel' (*Problem of the Hexateuch*, pp. 166-204; translated from *Archiv für Kulturgeschichte* 32, Weimar, 1944, pp. 1-42), p. 204.
[18] J. Lindblom, 'Wisdom in the Old Testament Prophets', VT Suppl. 3, pp. 192-204.
[19] E.g. J. Malfroy, 'Sagesse et loi dans le Deutéronome', *VT* 15, 1965, pp. 49-65; M. Weinfeld, 'The Origin of the Humanism in Deuteronomy', *JBL* 80, 1961, pp. 241-247.
[20] E. Gerstenberger, 'Covenant and Commandment', *JBL* 84, 1965, pp. 38-51.
[21] H. Brunner, 'Die Weisheitsliteratur', *Handbuch der Orientalistik*, ed. B. Spuler and others, Band I, Abschnitt 2, 1952, pp. 109f.
[22] *Art. cit.*   [23] *Art. cit.* See also Scott, *op. cit.*, p. xxxiii.

that Solomon composed proverbs and songs, and that 'he spoke of trees . . . , of beasts, and of birds, and of reptiles, and of fish' means that he compiled classified lists of natural phenomena in the manner of Egyptian onomastica and Babylonian word lists, but that the idea of composing these in poetic and gnomic form was his own personal contribution.

Since von Rad's important study of the Joseph Narrative,[24] we now know that wisdom teaching also affected narrative literature: the Joseph Narrative, whose strong affinities with Proverbs show it to be a product of the 'Solomonic enlightenment', is a 'didactic wisdom story which leans heavily upon influences emanating from Egypt, not only with regard to its conception of an educational ideal, but also in its fundamental theological ideas.'[25] Here also we have an example of the mingling of literary genres, in this case one which is not entirely without parallels in Egyptian literature.[26]

On the other hand it is generally admitted that the greatest literary achievement of the early monarchy lay in the field of historiography. At least two major works, generally reckoned as 'histories', were composed at this time: the Yahwist's history ('J') and the so-called Succession Narrative in the latter part of II Samuel and the first two chapters of I Kings. Both reflect the new national consciousness and confidence which the Davidic monarchy brought to Israel.[27] Von Rad[28] rightly saw in them both 'a recognition of the hidden activity of God in history' which is the product of reflexion upon the course of past events, culminating with the achievement of David. At first sight it would seem that wisdom influence is unlikely here: the writing of history on this scale was Israel's unique achievement, and its origins are already apparent in the sagas which the Yahwist incorporated into his work.[29] Neither in Egypt nor in any other part of the ancient near East do we find any historical work which can be seriously compared with the Israelite works in this field.

[24] See p. 4, n. 16 *supra*. For further details see pp. 76ff., *infra*.
[25] *Ibid.*, p. 300.   [26] See ch. 4, *infra*.
[27] G. von Rad, 'The Form-Critical Problem of the Hexateuch', in the work of the same name, pp. 50ff.; 'Beginnings', *ibid.*, pp. 203f.; *Theology I*, pp. 48ff.
[28] 'Beginnings', p. 203; 'Form-Critical Problem', p. 73.
[29] Von Rad, 'Beginnings', pp. 166-176.

Nevertheless we are entitled to ask whether a sharp distinction between the Joseph Narrative as a 'novel' and the Yahwistic history and Succession Narrative as 'history' is entirely legitimate. If the Joseph Narrative was composed at the same period, and in the same circles, as the Yahwistic History and the Succession Narrative, we might well expect to find that the wisdom tradition which influenced the former would not have been entirely without influence on the latter. All three works resemble one another in their concept of God as working in a hidden way through the hearts and minds of men, a concept which, in spite of the supposedly 'unhistorical' point of view of the Egyptian wisdom literature, nevertheless has a good deal in common with the 'God' of that tradition; and all are markedly superior to earlier Israelite saga in technical skill and treatment of character. All are to some degree works of the imagination, and whether they are to be judged as 'history' or 'fiction' is a matter of degree. It is in any case improbable that the Joseph Narrative is entirely without a historical foundation, while on the other hand the other two works obviously fall short of 'scientific history' in the modern sense. Thus the clear dependence of the Joseph Narrative on the Egyptian wisdom tradition raises the question how far in the other two works also the sudden development in the doctrine of God and in technique and treatment of character may be due to the same influence.

Von Rad has already pointed the way to the discussion of this question. In the case of the Succession Narrative he suggested that the author's new understanding of the divine activity was connected with the fact that the Israelite court 'was a centre of international wisdom lore'[30]; and he elsewhere[31] recognized affinities between it and the Joseph Narrative in 'spiritual outlook', style and psychological treatment of the characters.

In this book an attempt is made to explore these questions further by a closer examination of certain aspects of the Succession Narrative. In the following chapters the answer is sought to the following questions:

1. What is the character and purpose of the Succession Narrative?
2. To what extent, if at all, does it show the influence of the wisdom tradition?

[30] *Ibid.*, p. 203. Cf. also McKenzie, *art. cit.*
[31] 'Joseph Narrative', pp. 292f.

3. To what extent, if at all, has it been influenced by non-Israelite literature?

4. What features may fairly be claimed as belonging to the native Israelite tradition, or as due to the genius of the author himself?

It is not the purpose of this study to re-open the much discussed literary-critical problems of the Succession Narrative, but it is necessary to define the scope of the work which will be assumed in the chapters which follow.

1. I accept the opinion of the majority of scholars that it comprises at least II Sam. 9-20 + I Kings 1-2 (apart from a few short passages mentioned below), and that II Sam. 21-24 lie outside it.[32]

2. I consider it probable that the beginning is missing,[33] but I am sceptical about the possibility of reconstructing it entirely or in part from other passages in I and II Samuel. Consequently such earlier material will not be considered in the discussion.

3. I believe that the only external source which the author has incorporated, apart from a few short annalistic notices, is the account of the Ammonite War, comprising probably II Sam. 10.1-11.1a; 12.26-31. This source will be omitted from the discussion of the literary character of the work.

4. II Sam. 12.1-15. The Parable of Nathan (vv. 1-7a) seems to me to be a necessary part of the work.[34] But of the three pronouncements of punishment (vv. 7b-10, 11f., 13b-14) it is possible that the first two are not original, as they lack the subtlety which is characteristic of this writer.[35]

5. I Kings 2. This chapter presents many literary problems,[36] and theories of interpolation are almost as numerous as the scholars who have considered the question. It may be that the whole chapter has been reworked in such a way that the original version can no longer be discerned. But there are very few indications of this in the style, treatment of characters and point of

[32] See O. Eissfeldt, *The Old Testament: An Introduction*, Oxford, 1965, pp. 271ff. for a summary of discussion of the literary-critical problems.

[33] This is the view of L. Rost, 'Die Überlieferung von der Thronnachfolge Davids', *Das kleine Credo und andere Studien zum alten Testament*, Heidelberg, 1965, pp. 119-253. This work was originally published in BWANT III 6, 1926.

[34] For the contrary view see A. Lods, *Histoire de la littérature hébraïque et juive*, Paris, 1950, p. 160; Eissfeldt, *Introduction*, p. 272.

[35] So H. W. Hertzberg, *I and II Samuel* (OTL), 1964, *ad loc.*; Rost, *op. cit.*, p. 204; von Rad, 'Beginnings', p. 179.

[36] The most recent discussion is that of Noth, *Könige, ad loc.*

view. The only verses which are clearly not original are 2b-4, 27 (Deuteronomistic); 10f. (annalistic). The remainder of the chapter will therefore be included in the discussion.

II

THE CHARACTER AND PURPOSE OF
THE SUCCESSION NARRATIVE

PROBABLY no part of the Old Testament has received such consistent and unqualified praise as has the Succession Narrative. Since at least the days of Wellhausen, who praised it both for its historical reliability and for its understanding of human motives,[1] scholars have vied with one another in their use of superlatives in describing it. The enthusiasm of R. H. Pfeiffer, who asserted that it is 'a masterpiece, unsurpassed in historicity, psychological insight, literary style, and dramatic power',[2] whose 'vivid descriptions and characterizations and . . . lively dialogues have seldom if ever been surpassed in the literature of mankind',[3] is confirmed in its essentials by the more sober judgment of von Rad, who described it as 'historical writing . . . mature and artistically fully developed to an extent which makes it impossible to envisage further development in this direction'[4]; and similar views have been expressed by many other writers.[5]

This unqualified praise has been awarded to the author on three counts: as a historian, a psychologist and a literary genius. Concerning the last two, agreement has been virtually unanimous. In particular the three major studies of the book by Bernhard Luther, Rost and von Rad[6] all emphasize the same literary and psychological qualities which mark the author out as a writer of great sophistication far exceeding that of the authors of the sagas and popular narratives of the Old Testament.

Eissfeldt characterized the work as a '*good* historical novel'.[7] It is difficult to disagree with this judgment: the theme is historical,

---

[1] J. Wellhausen, *Prolegomena to the History of Israel*, Edinburgh, 1885, p. 262.

[2] R. H. Pfeiffer, *Introduction to the Old Testament*, New York, 1948, p. 357.

[3] *Ibid.*, p. 359.   [4] 'Beginnings', p. 193.

[5] E.g. Bernhard Luther in E. Meyer, *Die Israeliten und ihre Nachbarstämme*, Halle, 1906, pp. 189ff.; Lods, *op. cit.*, pp. 160ff.

[6] B. Luther in E. Meyer, *op. cit.*; Rost, *op. cit.*; von Rad, 'Beginnings'.

[7] *Introduction*, p. 141. In the German editions the word used is not *Novelle* but *Roman*, i.e. a novel in the modern sense. The italics are Eissfeldt's.

the treatment that of the novelist. But the term 'historical novel' is imprecise: its meaning depends upon the degree of emphasis which is placed respectively on the adjective and the noun. If the character of the book and its relationship with the cultural climate of its time are to be correctly assessed, it is necessary to investigate separately the claims which have been made for it, as a reliable historical work and as a work of the imagination.

1. *The Succession Narrative as history*

There is almost universal agreement that the author was a con-temporary, or near-contemporary, of David and a member of the court, who was therefore in an excellent position to write an authentic history of the reign.[8] Beyond this, the claim that he was an objective historian rests mainly on two grounds: that in spite of an obvious admiration for David he does not conceal his faults,[9] and that he almost never directly states his own opinion of actions or personalities, but lets them speak for themselves.[10] Other writers stress his qualities as an interpretative historian, drawing attention to his skill in arranging his material into a connected and significant story which reveals both the meaning of the historical events, the chain of cause and effect which links them together, and the nature of the historical process itself.[11]

Some writers have, however, expressed reservations. Well-hausen qualified his favourable estimate of the book's 'essentially historical character' by the remark that the author's narrow range of interest—the court life of Jerusalem—led him to ignore the wider national aspects of the events which he narrates.[12] A more recent writer[13] has maintained that the work is a moral tract in which the author's concern to warn the reader of the evil conse-quences of sin has outweighed all other considerations.

[8] So, apart from authors already cited, E. Auerbach, *Wüste und gelobtes Land* I, Berlin, 1932, p. 24; J. A. Montgomery and H. S. Gehman, *The Books of Kings* (ICC), 1951, p. 67; W. McKane, *I and II Samuel* (TC), 1963, pp. 19ff.; Hertzberg, *op. cit.*, p. 379.

[9] E.g. Wellhausen, Auerbach, von Rad.

[10] E.g. von Rad, 'Beginnings', p. 195.

[11] So E. Jacob, 'Histoire et historiens dans l'ancien testament', *RHPR* 35, 1955, pp. 28f.; A. Weiser, *Introduction to the Old Testament*, London, 1961, p. 66; McKane, *op. cit.*, p. 19.

[12] *Op. cit.*, p. 262.

[13] Morton Smith, 'The So-Called "Biography of David" in the Books of Samuel and Kings', *HTR* 44, 1951, pp. 167-169.

Others have seen in the very literary excellence of the book
reasons for questioning its historical accuracy. Rost,[14] while of
the opinion that the author would hardly have dared to invent
such an incident as David's adultery with Bathsheba (II Sam.
11.2-5) since he would have been open to refutation from others
who knew it to be untrue, nevertheless emphasized that artistic
motives are so intertwined with the history that a very careful
study would be required to distinguish between the two.

Some such attempt had in fact already been made by B. Luther,
some of whose conclusions have more recently been confirmed
by Eissfeldt. Luther[15] used the word *Novelle*, 'short story', of this
and some other Old Testament narratives, and raised the question
whether the author's 'novelistic' interests and techniques did not
override his historical sense. He cited the use of the Ammonite
War narrative in II Sam. 10-12 as proof that the author was not
primarily interested in history at all: he used authentic historical
material here merely as a background and starting-point for the
presentation of his own story of David's adultery, which was of
central interest to him. While not entirely denying a historical
sense to the author, Luther considered the work to be a psychological novel dealing with human passions, and questioned the
wisdom of using it as a reliable historical source.

Eissfeldt also pointed out that many scenes, especially private
conversations such as that between Amnon and Tamar in the
former's bedroom (II Sam. 13.11-16) can only be 'embellishment
arising out of poetic fantasy',[16] and considered that the whole
work is 'artistic narrative' rather than an eyewitness account,
although he admitted that in general the author's imagination was
informed by 'a good knowledge of the historical reality and a
sober sense of what is possible'.

If the work is to be accepted as a work of history in something
like the modern sense, it must be judged by the standards which
are normally applied to modern works of history. The first test
which must be applied to any historical narrative is that of its
congruity with reliable external evidence. This crucial test, however, can hardly be applied in this case: external evidence for the
period is almost wholly lacking.

Chronologically the events described are, with the possible ex-

---

[14] Pp. 232f.   [15] *Op. cit.*, pp. 191, 198f.
[16] *Introduction*, p. 141.

ception of the Ammonite War in II Sam. 10-12, all later than those narrated in the earlier chapters of I and II Samuel. The Succession Narrative does, it is true, frequently refer to those earlier events: David's early struggles (II Sam. 19./), his friendship with Jonathan (9.1), his escape from Saul and his succession to the kingdom (12.7f.), his victory over the Philistines and other enemies (19.9) and other events and circumstances of his earlier career are mentioned, and many personages from his early days reappear (e.g. Joab, Nathan, Zadok, Abiathar) in the same roles and with recognizably the same characteristics; but these references and signs of continuity merely provide the historical circumstances in which the Succession Narrative is set: they shed no light on the historicity of the later events which it describes. The undated stories in the appendix to II Samuel (chs. 21-24) also shed no light on the Succession Narrative, with the exception of the statement in 21.7 that David spared the life of Jonathan's son Meribbaal when he handed over the rest of Saul's descendants to be killed by the Gibeonites. This story appears to be related in some way to 9.1ff., which tells of David's desire to show kindness to any of Saul's house who may have remained alive. Shimei's curse in 16.7f. may also contain a reference to the story in 21.1ff.

The only other biblical source which tells the story of David's reign is I Chronicles. The Chronicler, however, completely omitted every scrap of material contained in the Succession Narrative. This fact neither confirms nor throws doubt upon the historicity of the latter, since it is generally accepted that the Chronicler's omissions from his written sources, which included the Books of Samuel and Kings, signify rather that he found these passages unsuited to his purpose than that he believed them to be unhistorical. In this case he may have felt that the events narrated in this part of II Samuel and I Kings did not present either David or Solomon in a sufficiently favourable light.[17]

There is, then, no means of checking the historical accuracy of the Succession Narrative by comparison with other biblical sources. The same may be said of extra-biblical sources. Apart from the account of the Ammonite War, the book contains almost no allusions to events outside David's empire, and none which can be checked.

[17] See Eissfeldt, *Introduction*, p. 532 for a representative opinion on this point.

The inapplicability of the first test of historical accuracy is by no means an unusual situation: comparatively few of the narratives in the Books of Kings, apart from those which refer to foreign policy and wars, can be checked in this way. The student of the historical narratives of the Old Testament is frequently forced, as in this case, to fall back on the secondary test of general probability: events are generally held to be basically historical when they are not inherently improbable, when they are congruent with the general course of history and of social, political and religious circumstances known to us, and when we can discern no probable motive which the author might have had for inventing or seriously distorting the facts.

If we apply these tests to the Succession Narrative, we may properly conclude that the public events there narrated are in general historical. Apart from the story of the Ammonite War which is essentially an extract from a reliable source, we may assume the historicity of at least the following events: David's marriage to Bathsheba, the widow of a Hittite officer named Uriah, shortly after her first husband had been killed in the Ammonite War; the death of their first child and the survival of their second, whom they named Solomon; the rape of Tamar, the murder of Amnon by Absalom and his consequent banishment; his recall, partial reconciliation with his father, and rebellion; David's flight from Jerusalem, his rally, his victory over Absalom's forces, and Absalom's death; the rebellion of Sheba; the abortive attempt of Adonijah to make himself king when David was in his dotage; the failure of Adonijah's plot and the successful proclamation of Solomon as king; the death of David and the subsequent steps taken by Solomon to do away with those whom he felt to be a danger to him. These bare facts, and possibly a few others, were events of public importance which can hardly have been unknown to the populace, and can therefore hardly have been invented by an author writing less than a generation after their occurrence.

But these are only the bare bones of the Succession Narrative. If the narrative of the latter part of David's reign had confined itself to the bald narration of these events, there would be little reason to doubt its historical reliability. It would in fact closely resemble many other narratives in the Books of Kings, which tantalize the reader by giving him little or no information about causes and motives, or about the feelings of those concerned, e.g. 'And they made a conspiracy against him in Jerusalem, and he fled to Lachish. But they sent after him to Lachish, and slew him there' (Amaziah, II Kings 14.19); 'In his days Pharaoh Necho king of Egypt went up to the king of Assyria to the river Euphrates. King Josiah went to meet him; and Pharaoh Necho slew him at Megiddo, when he saw him' (II Kings 23.29). But it is precisely the unique characteristic of the Succession Narrative that, at any rate without any overt tendentious motive, such as we may find in saga or in some theologically oriented narratives, it fills out these bare bones with the most detailed and subtle indications of the characters, motives and feelings of those who participated in the events which it describes, taking the reader for this purpose into corners and private rooms to spy upon secret meetings and to listen to intimate and secret conversations.

Some of the conversations which it records, such as the audiences which David granted to Ziba and Meribbaal (II Sam. 9) and his conversations with Uriah (11.7-12), Absalom (13.24-26), the woman of Tekoa (14.4-20) and Joab (14.21f.), are represented as having taken place in public or semi-public sessions of the court, and so might have been heard and remembered by a comparatively large number of people. But the book also abounds in completely intimate conversations and scenes: Nathan's private rebuke of David (12.1-15), Jonadab's advice to Amnon concerning the best way to seduce Tamar (13.3-5), the rape of Tamar (13.10-19) and the subsequent chance meeting of Absalom with his sister (13.20), Joab's conversation with Absalom after the latter had set fire to his field (14.31f.), Joab's plain words to David after the defeat of Absalom (19.5-7), the plot between Nathan and Bathsheba to secure the throne for Solomon (I Kings 1.11-14). The list could be extended.

The question at issue is not whether the author, like many another ancient historian, has used his imagination and his literary art to embellish and add dignity to actual conversations and speeches which in reality were simple and artless. That he did this is quite obvious: the series of speeches on the occasion of David's departure from Jerusalem (II Sam. 15.19-16.14) no doubt represents something which actually took place, yet this is clearly not a verbatim report. Similarly there was no doubt a council of war held by Absalom on his arrival in Jerusalem to assume the kingship, but the report of it in 16.15-17.14 is clearly a literary piece. This, however, is not the issue before us. The question is whether in the reports of *secret conversations and scenes* the author can be said in any sense at all to have recorded historical events. This question is crucial, because it is almost entirely by means of these private scenes that he gives his interpretation of the characters and motives of the principal personages and of the chain of cause and event; it is here that he shows those qualities as a narrator and interpreter of a long and complex series of events which are the basis of his reputation as a writer and historian. Without these passages the work would have none of those qualities; yet it is precisely they which are most obviously based on the imagination rather than on knowledge.

At most, as Montgomery and Gehman suggested,[18] they might be based on court gossip. If the author had been a member of David's court, he would have been in possession of a liberal supply of stories on which he could draw; but it is difficult to conceive how he could have *known* what happened on these private occasions, however well placed he may have been. It matters little for our present purpose whether he wrote partially under the stimulus of court gossip or whether his only inspiration was his own imagination. Novels and gossip are equally products of the imagination. Even in the story of the seduction of Bathsheba and the murder of Uriah it is possible that we have no more than a literary version of common gossip based on the known facts of the death of Uriah, his widow's rather hasty second marriage to the king and the death of their first child. We cannot be sure, with Rost, that the author 'would not have dared' to publish such a story if it were not true.

Another circumstance which leads us to doubt whether the Succession Narrative can properly be called a historical work is that, while the author lets us into many secrets about private motives, the public and political aspects of David's reign are extremely meagrely dealt with.[19] His work covers a period of something like twenty years: when it opens, David is still in the prime of life and Solomon not yet born; but it ends with the death of David as an old man and the accession of Solomon, evidently

[18] *Op. cit.*, p. 70.
[19] Cf. Wellhausen, *loc. cit.*; B. Luther, *op. cit.*, p. 196; Montgomery and Gehman, p. 70; Morton Smith, *art. cit.*, p. 169; Jacob, *art. cit.*, p. 30.

already a young man. Yet nothing is recorded of the public events of the reign after the establishment of the empire except the rebellions of Absalom and Sheba and the abortive attempt, at the end of David's life, of Adonijah to seize the throne. But it is hardly credible that there should have been nothing else of interest to report. David's achievements in peace, as in war, cannot have been inconsiderable, nor can the political problems have been negligible. The task of administering and maintaining the heterogeneous empire must have required great administrative sagacity. Nor can the reign have been almost wholly without incident, as the author implies. He records in detail—evidently because of its literary and psychological possibilities—one great series of events: the rebellion of Absalom, which nearly cost the king his throne, and its causes and consequences; but even here he has so insisted on one cause of it—the frustration and ambition of Absalom (II Sam. 13.34-15.6)—that he has almost entirely neglected the more solid political circumstances without which a single discontented prince could never have succeeded in gaining the massive support which he must have had. Fortunately for the modern historian, there are a few indirect references to these factors. A few passages hint at the reasons for the rising of the northern tribes (15.2-5; 20.1); we learn of the continued existence of a party which remained loyal to Saul and regarded David as a usurper and murderer (16.3, 5, 8); we may read into the fact that Absalom chose Hebron for his proclamation as king (15.10) some hostility on the part of the Judaeans towards David for having slighted the ancient Judaean capital in favour of Jerusalem[20]; we may judge the extent of David's unpopularity by the fact that the supporters of Absalom are referred to as 'the men of Israel' or 'Israel' while David's supporters are simply 'the servants of David', and we may speculate, in the light of this, on the meaning of the statement that 'all the land wept' as David departed from Jerusalem (15.23). We may, with Alt,[21] pick up these fragments and construct from them a tentative picture of the tribal and political, and perhaps also the social circumstances

[20] So Auerbach, *op. cit.*, p. 247; B. Luther, *op. cit.*, p. 196; and a number of more recent writers.

[21] 'The Formation of the Israelite State in Palestine', *Essays in Old Testament History and Religion*, Oxford, 1966, pp. 171-237; translated from *Kleine Schriften zur Geschichte des Volkes Israel* II, 1959, pp. 1-65; originally published in 1930, pp. 228ff.

which made possible the revolts of Absalom and Sheba; but the fact remains that the author has not presented them clearly: that he was not, in fact, interested in them. The hints which he has left were left unintentionally: he could not have told his story without mentioning them.

We may be sure that this author, who in dealing with private and personal matters shows himself to be unusually capable of making the nexus of cause and effect clear to the reader, could have done the same with regard to public events if he had wished to do so. Instead, he has left his readers in ignorance concerning the underlying causes of these revolts. This so-called historian of the latter part of the reign of David simply does not provide us with the material for understanding this vital period in which undoubtedly lay the seeds of future events: both the magnificence of the reign of Solomon and the sudden collapse which followed it. Everything has been subordinated to the personal element: to the characters and motives of a few men.

It has been urged[22] that nevertheless the Succession Narrative is a historical document within the limits set by the author's own interests: it is a *court* history, a history of David's court. The principal argument put forward in support of this view is that both the situations and characters are 'true to life': human character is here portrayed in all its complexity and tragedy. That this is true will be argued in a later section of this book; but it does not necessarily make the Succession Narrative a work of history. These traits are more frequently to be found in a good novel than in a work of history. The historian is rarely, if ever, in a position where he can do more than guess the motives of historical characters; the novelist, on the other hand, is free to construct his characters on the basis of observation of human nature in general. It may indeed be argued that the characters in the Succession Narrative are too human to be true: they are almost always placed in situations calculated above all else to show now one, now another side of their nature. It is unlikely that any history, confined as it must be to the recording of facts and of facts only, would be able to do this as perfectly as does the Succession Narrative.

[22] E.g. by S. R. Driver, *Introduction to the Old Testament*, Edinburgh, 1909, p. 182; C. R. North, *The Old Testament Interpretation of History*, London, 1946, p. 34; Weiser, *op. cit.*, p. 165.

We are therefore forced to conclude that the Succession Narrative, although its theme is an historical one and it makes use of historical facts, is not a work of history either in intention or in fact. The author's interests lay elsewhere.

2. *The Succession Narrative as a novel*

It has already been suggested in the foregoing discussion that the author has some of the qualities of the novelist. This suggestion must now be examined more closely. The claim that the work is a novel implies that it is the earliest work of its kind in Israelite literature: neither the earlier sagas, which belong rather to the category of popular narrative, nor the contemporary Yahwistic history, which is a composite work largely dependent on earlier sources, can be so called. As a narrative work of considerable length and complexity which is a free composition rather than dependent on older sources, the Succession Narrative stands by itself. This means that the claim that it is basically a novel can only be assessed by the standards which are applied by modern literary criticism to the novel of our own day.[23]

Among the most important features which we expect to find in a novel are the following: an essential unity of theme and action, leading—however diversified may be the subordinate themes—step by step to a logical and satisfactory conclusion; a structural unity, in which each chapter constitutes a distinct, vivid and realistic scene, yet plays an essential part in the whole; convincing and lively dialogue; credible characters, corresponding in their complexity to the experienced realities of human nature; and a lively and flexible style capable of conveying to the reader mood, feelings, atmosphere, irony and humour.

(a) *Unity of theme.* Without anticipating later discussion of the purpose of the book, we may define the central theme as that of the succession to the throne of David. As Rost[24] correctly pointed

---

[23] By 'novel' here is meant the classical novel as the word has been understood in the west since the eighteenth century: that is, the novel with a plot which is brought to a definite conclusion. It may be noted that the idea of comparing the Succession Narrative with the modern novel is not new: it is the basis of the literary criticism in the three major studies of B. Luther, Rost and von Rad—presumably because it is really the only method available to us.

[24] *Op. cit.*, pp. 194ff.

out, the clue to the whole work is to be found in I Kings 1 and 2, where it is made clear by constant reiteration of a kind of refrain:

'I *will be king*.' (Adonijah, 1.5)

'Have you not heard that Adonijah . . . *has become king* and David our lord does not know it?' (Nathan to Bathsheba, 1.11)

'Go in at once to King David, and say to him, "Did you not, my lord the king, swear to your maidservant, saying, 'Solomon your son *shall reign after me*, and he *shall sit upon my throne*'? Why then *is* Adonijah *king*?" ' (Nathan to Bathsheba, 1.13)

'My lord, you swore to your maidservant by Yahweh your God, saying, "Solomon your son *shall reign* after me, and he *shall sit upon my throne*." And now, behold, Adonijah *is king*, although you, my lord the king, do not know it.' (Bathsheba to David, 1.17f.)

'And now, my lord the king, the eyes of all Israel are upon you, to tell them who shall *sit on the throne* of my lord the king after him.' (Bathsheba to David, 1.20)

'My lord the king, have you said, "Adonijah *shall reign* after me, and he *shall sit upon my throne*"?' (Nathan to David, 1.24)

'Has this thing been brought about by my lord the king and you have not told your servants who *should sit on the throne* of my lord the king after him?' (Nathan to David, 1.27)

'As I swore to you by Yahweh, the God of Israel, saying, "Solomon your son *shall reign* after me, and he *shall sit upon my throne* in my stead"; even so will I do this day.' (David to Bathsheba, 1.30)

'He shall come and *sit upon my throne*, for he *shall be king* in my stead.' (David, 1.35)

'Solomon *sits upon the royal throne*.' (Jonathan to Adonijah, 1.46)

'Blessed be Yahweh, the God of Israel, who has granted one of my offspring to *sit upon my throne* this day.' (David, 1.48)

So Solomon *sat upon the throne* of David his father. (2.12)

So *the kingdom was established* in the hand of Solomon. (2.46b)

Working back from these last chapters, Rost had no difficulty in demonstrating that this theme which is expressed so insistently at the end of the book is in fact its central theme. Every incident in the story without exception is a necessary link in a chain of narrative which shows how, by the steady elimination of the alternative possibilities, it came about that it was Solomon who succeeded his father on the throne of Israel.

The book begins with a narrative (II Sam. 9) which reminds the reader of the still existing threat to the new dynasty of a restoration of the house of Saul.[25] The purpose of bringing Meribbaal on the scene at this point is to prepare for the narratives (16.1-4; 19.24-30) where the reader is deliberately left in doubt over the loyalty of Meribbaal at the time of Absalom's rebellion; and the incidents involving Shimei, 'a man of the family of the house of Saul' (16.5-14; 19.16-23; I Kings 2.8f., 36-46), together with the revolt of Sheba, who was a member of Saul's tribe of Benjamin (II Sam. 20), remind the reader of the latent possibility which continued to exist throughout David's reign, that David would not have *any* successor to sit on his throne; and they show how this danger was fought against and eventually eliminated.

Chapters 10-12 then take up a different aspect of the succession theme: the origins of the man who did in fact succeed David, i.e. Solomon. This necessitated the introduction of an account of the war against the Ammonites which formed the background to the story of the birth of Solomon; and here the author decided, contrary to his usual custom, to incorporate more or less unchanged into his book narratives which he took from a contemporary annalistic source: 10.1-11.1a; 12.26-31. The series of events which is inserted between these two annalistic excerpts is of vital importance for the development of the main theme. Bathsheba, here introduced for the first time, not only became the mother of David's eventual successor, but was later to play a decisive role in securing the throne for her son through her influence over David in his senility (I Kings 1.11-31). Through the account of the birth and premature death of her first son by David, who, if he had lived, would have been a candidate for the throne (11.27; 12.15ff.), followed by the notice of the birth of her second son Solomon, of whom it is said that 'Yahweh loved him' (12.24), the reader's attention is drawn to the problem of

---

[25] If Rost is right in believing II Sam. 6.16, 20-23; 7.11b, 16 to be part of a lost beginning of the book, this theme emerges all the more clearly: if Michal had not been barren, the two houses might have been united in the person of a son, who would have been the son of David and the grandson of Saul; but this was made impossible by Michal's barrenness.

the succession, whose solution is already suggested in a veiled way. Meanwhile the story of David's adultery, revealing his emotional instability, has prepared the way for the account of his later ineptitude in personal matters, which was also to prove to be a vital element in the elimination of Absalom from the succession.

After this introduction, Bathsheba and her son retire into the background, and the remainder of the work, with the exception of II Sam. 20, is devoted to the rival candidates for the throne, Solomon's half-brothers Amnon, Absalom and Adonijah, and their elimination, leaving the field clear for the triumph of Solomon at the very end. The story of Amnon's rape of his half-sister Tamar (13.1-19) leads to his elimination from the succession through his murder by Absalom, and the latter action in turn introduces the series of events which led to Absalom's rebellion (13.20-38). With the death of Amnon and the banishment of Absalom it appears that *two* of the rival candidates have now been eliminated; but then begins (ch. 14) the account of Absalom's return from banishment and partial reconciliation with his father, a story which gives yet another twist to the succession theme, while explaining the circumstances which led to his rebellion. The story of the rebellion itself and its defeat (chs. 15-19) shows not only how precarious was David's own position, but also how the succession question came near to being solved in an entirely unexpected way.

In the course of this story the incidents involving Shimei and Meribbaal, who is credited by Ziba with having tried to take advantage of the confusion of the times to assert his own claim to the throne (16.3), once more remind the reader of the continued threat from the house of Saul. At the end of ch. 19, with the rebellion quelled and Absalom dead, the succession question is still unsolved; and before the final solution which comes as the result of Adonijah's unsuccessful coup, the story of Sheba's rebellion (ch. 20) raises pertinently the question—which is related to that of the claims of the house of Saul—of the extent of the kingdom which is to be inherited. The question is now not of an usurpation of the whole kingdom but whether the kingdom will be redivided into two parts, with the north reverting to Benjamite rule, leaving to David's successor a greatly impoverished kingdom. With this question settled by the collapse of Sheba's rebellion and the death of the pretender, the stage is now set for the final act.

We are now introduced to the remaining rival candidate, Adonijah, who attempts to take advantage of his aged father's apparent incapacity either to control events or to settle the now urgent question of the succession, by proclaiming himself king. This had the effect of stirring the supporters of Solomon into action, and gave them the weapon which they needed to force David into a decision. The story now rapidly reaches its conclusion with the anointing and enthronement of Solomon, the flight of Adonijah, the death of David, and finally the statement that 'Solomon sat upon the throne of his father; and his kingdom was firmly established' (I Kings 2.12). The remainder of the work is, as Rost noted,[26] a kind of appendix, though not an irrelevant one, describing the measures taken by Solomon to make his position completely secure.

The work is, then, a unity in which each scene is essential to the whole and to the development of the central theme of the succession.[27] But it is not only the central theme which gives the story its unity. A number of subordinate themes running through it make their contribution. Of these the most important is the psychological study of the family history of David, with its interpretation of the personal disasters which befell him and his sons as the consequence of his own weakness of character.[28] This theme is most clearly expressed in two of Nathan's words spoken when he condemned David's seduction of Bathsheba and murder of Uriah: 'Now therefore the sword shall never depart from your house' (II Sam. 12.10), and: 'Behold, I will raise up evil against you out of your own house; and I will take your wives before your eyes, and give them to your neighbour, and he shall lie with your wives in the sight of this sun' (12.11). The fact that these words may not be an original part of the narrative is of no consequence: even if this is so, they are additions made by a reader who has correctly—though with more overt piety and less subtlety than the author normally shows—discerned the theme in question and expressed it in plain words for the benefit

[26] P. 194.
[27] This point was recognized by writers earlier than Rost, e.g. by S. R. Driver, *Introduction*, p. 183.
[28] Cf. the comment by H. A. Leimbach, quoted by Hertzberg, *op. cit.*, p. 378: 'Chapters 11-20 might be called "David's sin and its consequences".'

SN C

of readers who might not be sufficiently subtle to discover it for themselves. The theme is undoubtedly present in the original narrative: although the death of the first child born to the murderer and his victim's wife is the direct punishment for the murder (12.13-15), that death is only the prelude to a horrifying series of calamities which befall David and his other children and household: the rape of Tamar, the public humiliation of David's concubines by his own son, the rebellion of two of his sons and the violent deaths of two of them—Amnon and Absalom—within their father's lifetime and of a third—Adonijah—soon afterwards. The pathos and tragedy of these events and their crippling effect on David's character are clearly brought out in the scene in which David mourns for Absalom (II Sam. 18.33-19.8). This theme of a man forced throughout his remaining years to witness in his own family the effects of that same violence and lust of which he himself has been guilty is one which greatly contributes to the book's literary unity.

Other thematic threads run through the book: the Meribbaal story is in three parts (II Sam. 9; 16.1-4; 19.24-30), each part standing naturally in its own context, while the whole forms a distinct sub-plot. The tragic story of Joab forms another. The unity of the book is also reinforced by numerous subtle details which, to the discerning reader, evoke memories of earlier scenes or foreshadow later ones. Thus when Absalom cohabits with David's concubines (II Sam. 16.22) he does it 'on the roof', presumably that same 'roof of the king's house' from which his father had had his first fateful glimpse of Bathsheba (11.2). The words of the wise woman of Tekoa, when she speaks of the threat to her 'name and remnant' if both her sons are taken from her (14.7) are, in spite of David's promise that her second son will be spared, already looking forward to the death of Absalom, and epitomize the question of the dynastic succession. Again, the whole tragedy of Joab, the man who in the end pays with his life for having put loyalty to the interests of the State before other loyalties (19.1-8; I Kings 2.28ff.), is presaged in the scene in which his efforts to serve the State by reconciling Absalom and David receive as their only reward the destruction of his property by the man whose cause he has championed (II Sam. 14.29-33). Again, the series of tragedies in David's family is made more poignant by the constant references to the physical beauty of its members: Bathsheba, 11.2; Tamar, 13.1; Absalom, 14.25 and his daughter Tamar, 14.27; Adonijah, I Kings 1.6. These are also clearly intended to recall David's own physical beauty (I Sam. 16.12), which, although it is not mentioned in the Succession Narrative, was evidently well known to the reader.

Another unifying bond is the consistent treatment of the characters. From the moment when he first appears, each one (with the exception of the really minor ones) is kept in the author's mind, and his story is brought to a definite conclusion within the compass of the book. In some cases (Amnon, Absalom, Adonijah, Joab, Amasa, Shimei, Ahithophel) a man's career is followed through to a death which is directly related to his actions; in others there is some other definite conclusion: in the case of Abiathar, banishment and supersession by Zadok (I Kings 2.26); with Bathsheba and Nathan, who are regularly linked together in the narrative, it is the happy fulfilment, through the accession of Solomon, of a lifetime's ambition. With another pair, Ziba and Meribbaal, three scenes scattered through the book end with a compromise decision which nevertheless brings their tragicomedy to a conclusion. Even with such minor characters as Barzillai, the author is unwilling to leave an incident once begun (II Sam. 17.27-29; 19.31-40) without a definite conclusion (I Kings 2.7). As von Rad rightly saw,[29] these multiple threads which run intertwined through the book are a strong argument in favour of its unity.

(b) *Structure.* The division of the book into distinct scenes or chapters is to be understood in purely artistic terms. This is unusual in the Old Testament: in most of the narratives of comparable length the breaks in the story mark the points where an editor has joined two originally separate incidents together.[30] But the author of the Succession Narrative was entirely master of his own material, and had to solve for himself the problem of dividing it into vivid and artistically satisfactory scenes while maintaining continuity.[31] This he did with remarkable success, as

[29] 'Beginnings', pp. 191f.
[30] This is true, for example, of the stories of David's early career in the Books of Samuel. The main exceptions are the Joseph Narrative and the books of Ruth, Jonah and Esther.
[31] This independence of source material is widely accepted, e.g. by von Rad, 'Beginnings', p. 191, though Eissfeldt (*Introduction*, p. 139) questions it.

may be seen from an analysis of the account of the events which led to Absalom's rebellion, II Sam. 13.1-15.12.

Absalom is introduced for the first time in 13.1; by 15.12 his rebellion has been launched, and David's throne and life are in danger. From a quiet and apparently unpromising statement that 'Absalom, David's son, had a beautiful sister whose name was Tamar', the author leads the reader through a series of scenes in which the tension steadily increases, to the climax of 15.10-12. Notes on the passage of time amounting to eleven years (13.23, 38; 14.28; 15.7) remind us that we are witnessing a slow and inexorable process which has been compressed into a small compass. The choice of incidents, clearly revealing the change in Absalom's character and the growth of his inordinate ambition out of a sense of frustration and righteous indignation, is adroitly made. The scene changes frequently; but there are five main 'chapters': the rape of Tamar, 13.1-22; the murder of Amnon and Absalom's consequent banishment, 13.23-39; the attempts to secure his return, 14.1-33; the preparations for the rebellion, 15.1-6; and the climax, the act of rebellion itself, 15.7-12. Of these the third consists of two distinct but closely related scenes (14.1-24, 28-33) joined by an interlude (14.25-27). Each chapter is complete in itself and is brought to an appropriate conclusion; yet in each case the concluding words themselves unmistakably hint that this cannot be a final solution, but only marks a pause in the action which satisfies none of the participants. This sense of unease creates in the reader a new feeling of suspense, and so preserves the momentum of the story as a whole. There is a sense of inevitable movement towards some final crisis. Relief is given, however, to the monotony of a movement in one direction only by the device of departure and return, which is strikingly emphasized by the choice of words. In the second scene the word 'go' recurs insistently (13.24, 25 (twice), 26 (twice), 27), to be followed by the equally insistent repetition of words meaning 'flee' (vv. 29, 34, 37, 38). In the third these keywords are replaced first by 'bring back' (14.13, 21, 23), then by 'dwell' (vv. 24, 28) and finally 'see the face (of the king)' (vv. 24, 28, 32). At each step there is suspense; and the gradual approach of the once banished Absalom back towards the centre of events hints at the final step, when he will for a time succeed in placing himself in the very centre itself.

Ostensibly the central character in these chapters is Absalom; yet in a deeper sense the reader is made to feel that it is David whom the author seeks to portray: David who is in a true sense the architect of Absalom's destiny—the one who gave him life, who gave him his inherited qualities of impetuosity and cunning, ambition and ruthlessness; who was ultimately responsible, through the ineptitude of his treatment of him, weak and sentimental, yet hesitant, for his final fatal venture. Throughout these chapters the figure of David looms like an evil genius over the protagonists.

In each chapter the central action is described with dramatic terseness: 13.14; 13.29; 14.13; 14.30; 15.10. The author's real interest lies not in the actions themselves but in their causes, circumstances and consequences. It is especially in the concluding sections that one may observe how his chapters are rounded off as distinct units, while at the same time pointing forward to further developments. In 13.1-22, the personal tragedy of Tamar is complete in v. 20b; but verses 21f., which describe the new state of affairs (David angry, Absalom nursing hatred for Amnon, Amnon thus in danger) create a new tension. Action is suspended; but the future is uncertain.

Similarly in 13.23-39, the action is completed, it would seem, in v. 38: Tamar is avenged, and all three participants in the drama have been removed from the scene, Amnon by death, Tamar by disgrace and Absalom by flight. Yet the final words make it clear that things cannot remain in this state: David longs for reconciliation with his son (v. 39); and so the reader is prepared for the next chapter.

Again in 14.1-24 the return of Absalom to Jerusalem (vv. 23, 24a) seems to have brought the story to a close; but the final words (v. 24b) that 'he did not see the king's face' again show that the solution can only be a temporary one.

At this point (14.25-27) the author uses the pause to introduce a passage describing Absalom's handsome appearance which can hardly be presented in narrative form but is necessary as a prelude to a later scene (15.1-6) in which Absalom is to 'steal the hearts of the men of Israel' (15.6). The reference to Absalom's daughter Tamar, who was beautiful like her unfortunate namesake, seems to be intended to point forwards as well as backwards: for Absalom, the incident of his sister's humiliation is not over, and will never be over: he bears a grudge against his father which will drive him on to even more desperate action. The insertion of this descriptive passage into a narrative packed with incident also serves to create suspense, and to draw the reader's attention to the fact that from now on it is Absalom who will be at the centre of events.

14.28-33, which begins with a reminder of the unsatisfactory situation of Absalom on his return to Jerusalem, seems at first sight to end happily: the king signifies publicly his reconciliation with his son (v. 33). Yet this is in fact the 'calm before the storm': Absalom's preparations for rebellion, unhurried though they are (15.7), begin from this point. If we look more closely at the final verse it will be seen that here also the author has introduced an ominous note, the most subtle of all: the scene is enacted in total silence. Elsewhere we are told without restraint about David's emotions at times of crisis: he was angry (13.21); he rent his garments (13.31); he wept bitterly (13.36); he longed for Absalom (13.39); he mourned bitterly over Absalom's death (18.33; 19.4). Yet at this moment we are told nothing. Absalom had forced his father's hand, the interests of the State required a formal reconciliation, and David bowed to those interests; but the reconciliation was no more than formal. The author has told us plainly by his silence how cold and formal was that kiss. There were now, he implies, two rivals for the throne. This was the moment when Absalom realized that there was now nothing more to be expected from his father. So 14.33 leads the perceptive reader to expect a dénouement of the whole story; and it comes in 15.1-12.

So chs. 13-15 provide clear proof that the 'scenes' in this work are not, as elsewhere in Old Testament narrative, the result of the joining of sources by an editor but literary units within an original work, created for purely literary and artistic reasons. The other parts of the book confirm this.

The first chapters (II Sam. 9-12) are somewhat less perfect from the literary point of view, partly because the author has here used an older source and partly because the beginning of the work is lost. Nevertheless the same techniques can be seen. The story of Meribbaal (9.1-13) is broken off at a point which offers a conclusion of a kind; yet that very conclusion—lame Meribbaal dependent on a servant whose trustworthiness has not been men-

tioned; a descendant of Saul installed at court—suggests the
possibility, if not the certainty, of further development, which is
in fact found later in the story (16.1-4). Similarly the story of
David and Bathsheba (11.2 12.25) is a preparatory chapter which
finds its sequel at the very end of the work in I Kings 1.11ff.,
when the same four persons, David, Bathsheba, Nathan and
Solomon, gather all the themes together with the accession of
Solomon to the throne, a sequel hinted at in the final verses of
the first story (12.24f.), where Solomon is named Jedidiah,
'Yahweh's beloved'. These two stories provide a framework for
the stories concerning the fate of David's other children.

In the account of Absalom's rebellion (15.13-19.40), the
literary problems were quite different, and the methods corres-
pondingly so. The problem in 13.1-15.12 was to trace the fate of
Absalom over a long period of time in such a way as to show not
only the relationship between the events but also the gradual
change in Absalom's character, its causes and its consequences.
This task required the selection of a number of scenes, each of
which should be complete in itself yet organically related to the
whole. The events of 15.13-19.40 cover only, at most, a few weeks,
and describe a single event: Absalom's rebellion. The subject
provided the author both with opportunities and with technical
problems. The main character was now once again David, at one
of the greatest crises of his life; and thus the opportunity was
provided of depicting aspects of his character not previously
brought out. This the author did principally by creating a number
of short scenes (15.13-16.14; 19.16-40) which depict David's relations with a host of people: David's servants and his personal
bodyguard, Ittai and his Gittites, the priests, Ahithophel, Hushai,
Meribbaal, Ziba, Shimei, Abishai. Each scene reveals some
aspect of David's character.

The technical problem, however, lay elsewhere, in the ordering
of the narrative. It was necessary that each side of the conflict
should receive equal attention, and this involved a dove-tailing
of two sets of scenes, those concerning Absalom and those concerning David. This had to be done without confusing or losing
the attention of the reader, and it had never been done satis-
factorily before in Hebrew narrative. The author chose to do it
by inserting a single block of narrative about Absalom and his
followers (16.15-17.14) into a main narrative which is told from

David's point of view. He inserted it into a natural pause in the
story, when David and his men had reached the Jordan, safe
from immediate pursuit, and were resting (16.14). At this point
the reader would naturally wonder how safe David was there,
and would wish to know what Absalom was doing. The change
of scene is therefore entirely appropriate. Similarly, at the end of
the block of narrative about Absalom, the reader is led back to
David's camp quite naturally through the story of David's spies
in Jerusalem—already prepared for in 15.32-37—as they themselves return to David with news (17.15-22). From this point,
after a short description of the disposition of the forces on both
sides (17.24-26) it was possible to tell the rest of the story from
the point of view of David, including in it the battle and the
death of Absalom.

The story of the revolt of Sheba (ch. 20), an event which
followed closely upon that of Absalom, presented no difficulties
to the author.

After this[32] there occurs one of the major breaks in the narrative
(cf. 10.1; 13.1). The author apparently was uninterested in any
events which may have occurred between the revolt of Sheba
and Adonijah's abortive attempt on the throne. The story of the
ministry of Abishag to David in his old age (I Kings 1.1-4) is a
transitional passage (cf. 14.25-27) which, although it in no sense
fills the chronological gap, serves the literary purpose by return-
ing the reader gently to the atmosphere of the court after the
military scenes of the previous chapters, while at the same time
providing the psychological atmosphere of a kingdom in perilous
waters, with the strong hand of the king no longer firmly on the
helm, and the king himself a prey to ambitious advisers.[33] The
link with previous events is made in 1.5-8: everything related
here about Adonijah reminds the reader of the earlier tragedy of
Absalom: the statement about his chariots and fifty runners (cf.
II Sam. 15.1), his personal beauty (cf. 14.25), and the ominous
statement that his father had spoiled him and never exercised
parental control over him (1.6). The parallel is then made explicit
by the mention of the name of Absalom in v. 6b. History, it

---

[32] II Sam. 20.22 was followed immediately in the original Succession
Narrative by I Kings 1.1: nothing has been omitted. See Noth, *Könige*, p. 8.
[33] The fact that the whole paragraph is circumstantial in character is suggested by the choice of an initial nominal clause in 1.1.

would seem, was about to repeat itself. Then in vv. 7f. the past is further recalled with a list of names which remind the reader of many previous episodes: Joab, Abiathar, Zadok, Nathan. The fact that these are now divided into two opposing camps leads the reader to expect the arrival of the final crisis of the story.

This concluding section of the work has a unity of theme, since it is the attempt of Adonijah which provokes the proclamation of Solomon; but like the Absalom story it is divided into chapters. There is a pause in 2.10-12 with the death of David and the accession of Solomon, and this might seem to be the end of the story, but for 1.53: the fact that Adonijah, after the failure of his attempt, should have been allowed to go on living as if nothing had happened, yet without a reconciliation with Solomon —another reminiscence of the Absalom story—has already persuaded the reader that there must be more to come. There are many loose strands left over; and it is not until the conclusion of ch. 2 that the end comes, with Solomon at last firmly settled on the throne (2.46b).

The technical craftsmanship which the author shows in the structure of his story and its division into chapters is seen also in the detailed handling of each chapter regarded as a unit. The art of constructing a story with an artistically satisfying form was not new: even the authors of the sagas of the patriarchs succeeded admirably in doing this.[34] Most of these stories, however, are relatively short and simple. Even in the case of longer and more complex stories, such as that of the mission of Abraham's servant to find a wife for Isaac (Gen. 24), where changes of scene were necessary, the narrator did not set himself any very taxing problems: all the events in that story, from the despatch of the messenger in vv. 2-9 to his return in vv. 62ff., are given in simple chronological order, and told from a single standpoint. In the Succession Narrative the author set himself problems of considerable complexity, and solved them with such dexterity that only the careful reader is aware of their existence. The scene often changes rapidly: for example, in II Sam. 13.1-22 the main events are set in Amnon's house; but there is considerable movement among the other characters: the king visits Amnon in his house, then sends a message to Tamar (v. 7); Tamar goes to Amnon's

[34] Cf. H. Gunkel, *Legends of Genesis*, recently reprinted in New York, 1964.

house; after Amnon's assault she is put out into the street, meets
Absalom there and is conducted by him to his house. Finally we
return to David, whose reaction is noted. In the second half of
the chapter, there is again rapid change of scene: the invitation
to the feast (v. 23), the interview with David (vv. 24-27), the
instructions to the servants (v. 28), the deed itself (v. 29a) and
the flight of the guests (29b). At this point a further complication
is introduced in order to create a situation of dramatic irony:
while the king's sons are actually on their way back to Jerusalem
with a true account of what has taken place (v. 30), a false rumour
that *all* the king's sons have been murdered reaches David.

Again, in II Sam. 18.19-33 the scene-changing is very rapid.
After the battle in which Absalom is defeated and killed, the question how the king is to be told arises. The author's desire to
create suspense and, once again, dramatic irony, involves a complicated narrative: the scene on the battlefield, with the despatch
in succession of the two runners (vv. 19-23), the double scene
between David, sitting in the gate, and the watchman on the roof
(vv. 24-27), and the arrival of the runners in the reverse order of
their setting out (already prepared for in vv. 23f.).

Perhaps the most complex passage in the whole work is
I Kings 1.1-53. The revolt of Adonijah, which led to the anointing
and proclamation of Solomon, is the climax of the whole book,
and the author was determined not only to show the chain of
cause and effect which brings the story to its conclusion, but also
to record its effects on several groups of people. The actual
dénouement occurs in ch. 2, but the events of that chapter are a
foregone conclusion. The climax is reached in ch. 1. The telling
of the story involved a number of different groups of people, and
a number of events or situations occurring more or less simul-
taneously in different places: Adonijah and his followers at
En-rogel, the old king isolated and impotent in his bedroom,
Nathan and Bathsheba plotting in the latter's palace, and the
anointing and proclamation of Solomon at Gihon, followed by
his enthronement in the throne-room in the palace. All these had
to be worked into a single, smooth narrative. This involved a
particularly complicated piece of dovetailing: from David's bedroom (vv. 1-4) the reader is transported to Adonijah's circle at
court (vv. 5-8) and then on to En-rogel, the scene of the rebellion
itself; the introduction of the next theme, Nathan's intrigue with

Bathsheba, takes us first to Bathsheba's palace (vv. 11-14) and then back to David's bedroom (vv. 15-37), out in procession to Gihon for Solomon's anointing (vv. 38-40) and then back to Adonijah at En-rogel, where the feast is still going on (vv. 41-48). Here the themes are drawn together by the arrival of a messenger who reports two more scenes: Solomon's enthronement in the throne-room (v. 46) and the congratulatory visit of David's servants to him, once again in his bedroom (v. 47), an important turning-point in the story which marks the disappearance of David as an effective force and his replacement by 'King Solomon'. The strands are finally pulled together with Adonijah's flight to the altar (v. 50) and the throne-room scene (v. 53) in which the confrontation of the two rivals takes place and Adonijah is dismissed to his house.

This story is technically perhaps the most complex story describing a single event in the Old Testament; yet the scenes have been so well dovetailed that the whole narrative reads smoothly and naturally, and the reader is at no time in any confusion or doubt about the sequence or coincidence of the events.[35] Occasionally the devices used to achieve this effect are visible, e.g. in v. 15, where a circumstantial clause reminds the reader of David's condition, already described in vv. 1-4. But in most cases the effect is obtained simply by a mastery of the art of narration which knows exactly when and where to make a change of scene. As a result we have as it were a panoramic view of the whole city of Jerusalem at that moment, in which can be seen the deeds, reactions and fates of a host of characters, including even the people (v. 40).

If we compare these narratives with even the most sophisticated of the narratives in the other historical books of the Old Testament, their superiority is evident. For example, in the story of David's farewell to Jonathan (1 Sam. 20), where the author had a fairly complicated story to tell, though less complicated than I Kings 1, the narration is technically so inept that the reader is often in confusion. Both the plan to let David know what happens at the feast (vv. 5-23) and its execution (vv. 35-40) are described in a confused way; moreover the author's desire, in addition, to include a touching and significant farewell scene (vv. 41f.) makes nonsense of the arrangement that Jonathan should communicate with David by a prearranged sign to avoid the risk of their being seen together. The account is so confused that it has been thought to be a conflation of two sources,[36] but this hypothesis, for which there is no real evidence, is insufficient to explain what are clearly blemishes on the part of an author whose mastery of his art was insufficient for the task which he had set himself: an imperfect control over complicated dialogue, inefficient scene-changing, and an inability to portray emotions without the creation of a special set piece as their vehicle.

Again, the story of Joseph's dealings with his brothers in Egypt (Gen. 42.6-45.15), although it does not lack psychological insight, is wooden, forced and unnatural at many points: the author is heavily dependent on the traditional devices of epic narrative or folk-tale, with their frequent repetition of incident and dialogue with only slight variations. Unlike I Sam. 20, its plot is relatively free from confusion, but the effort to create a logical and symmetrical plot has been achieved at the expense of credibility and resemblance to real life.

(c) *Use of dialogue*. This is one of the most striking features of the book. Elsewhere in the Old Testament dialogue is often used to reveal the characters and emotions of the speakers, often with considerable subtlety.[37] But in no other Old Testament narrative does the effectiveness of the stories depend so completely on dialogue as here. The dialogue in the Succession Narrative not only reveals character: it often bears the whole weight of the action, dispensing the author from the necessity of making his own comments about the motives of the speakers, a clumsy device to which he resorts only very rarely. Thus in the story of David and Uriah the Hittite (II Sam. 11.6-25) the narrator nowhere says that David first determined to cover up his adultery by bringing Uriah home on leave; that when this stratagem failed, he determined to kill him; that Joab was faced with a difficult assignment; that having carried it out, at the possible cost of his military reputation, he felt the need to defend himself by a kind of blackmail; that the message which he sent had to be carefully worded in order not to arouse the suspicion of the messenger. All this is subtly conveyed to the reader through the

[36] So, e.g., Hertzberg *ad loc*.
[37] E.g. the dialogues in Gen. 3.

conversations in vv. 8-12 (with the repeated 'Go down to your house'; 'Why did you not go down to your house?') and by David's letter (v. 15) and the conversations between Joab and the messenger and the messenger and David. No explanation by the narrator could so well have conveyed these complex motives, or indeed so well revealed the characters of Joab and David in such an entertaining way.

Again, the story of David's grief over the death of Absalom and of Joab's intervention at the risk of his own safety to save the situation by an apparently callous rebuke (18.33-19.8), which is one of the most revealing and moving episodes in the book, would be flat and uninteresting if it were told, as it could have been told, in the form of a direct narrative. As it is, it consists almost entirely of dialogue, which moves the reader by its realism and holds him in suspense concerning the outcome of such a bold and unexpected outburst, while it illuminates the whole book by revealing important aspects of the characters of David and Joab which are essential for an understanding of the whole inner history of these years.

Other examples of the use of dialogue could be given. Much of it is, of course, ordinary conversation necessary to any narrative work and comparable with dialogue in other Old Testament books; but it is in the intimate scenes, in which the spoken word predominates, and through which the clash of personalities can be seen, that the real superiority of the work lies. The formal speeches of Nathan (II Sam. 12.1-7), Ahithophel (17.1-3) and Hushai (17.8-13) are also masterpieces of their own kind.[38]

(d) *Portrayal of character.* As was pointed out by Rost[39] and reiterated by many later writers, artistically the most subtle and mature feature of the book is the author's treatment of character and his profound psychological insight. This is seen most clearly in the fully drawn major characters, although even the minor ones possess a life of their own.

David as portrayed in the Succession Narrative is the most fully delineated of all the characters in the Old Testament. The real greatness of this psychological study is measured by the fact that even so, he remains for the reader an essentially elusive

---

[38] On the speeches of Ahithophel and Hushai see pp. 57f., 83, *infra.*
[39] P. 231. See also von Rad, *Theology* I, p. 313.

personality. This is not due to any vagueness or inconsistency on the part of the author. On the contrary, it is the very richness and variety of his literary creation which raises the figure of David to a stature comparable with the great tragic heroes of literature. The character is drawn so close to life that we find it impossible to understand him fully, because he has the complexity of a real person. It is this enigmatic manner of his portrayal which has occasioned the expression of so many different views concerning the meaning and purpose of the Succession Narrative. In incident after incident we see more than one possible explanation of David's conduct. Was he really magnanimous to Meribbaal (II Sam 9.1-13), or was he merely being prudent in arranging to have him under his eye? And what of his piety? When he accepted the death of his child with the words 'But now he is dead; why should I fast? Can I bring him back again? I shall go to him, but he will not return to me' (12.23); when he sent the Ark back to Jerusalem with the words, 'Behold, here I am, let him do to me what seems good to him' (15.26); when he prevented Abishai from killing Shimei, saying, 'If he is cursing because Yahweh has said to him, "Curse David", who then shall say, "Why have you done so?"' (16.10)—was this genuine piety, or was it a calculated attempt to impress his followers? Are these further examples of David's well known cunning, such as he revealed when he sent Hushai back to Jerusalem to 'defeat the counsel of Ahithophel'? Here surely the author has deliberately left his readers in doubt.

Not only David's clemency and piety but even his greatness is similarly left an open question. David was, in the end, successful —though he had more than once come close to total failure—in the achievement of his political and military aims. He left behind him a strong kingdom and an assured succession. We are allowed to see some of the factors which contributed to this success: David's personal charm and his ability to command complete loyalty (especially in Joab, Ittai, Hushai); his craftiness, especially when hard pressed; his personal courage, as when he wanted to take the field in person against Absalom; his tactical skill and ability to come to a swift decision, as when he temporarily abandoned Jerusalem to Absalom. Yet over and over again, as king and statesman, he shows the most absurd ineptitude: though accustomed to the role of judge, he is unable to distinguish between a true and a fictitious story whether it is Nathan

(II Sam. 12.1-6) or the wise woman of Tekoa (14.1-11) who tells it; he is totally blind to the fact that Absalom is steadily undermining his position; he is incapable of seeing, until it is rudely pointed out to him by Joab (19.1-8) that his uncontrolled grief over the death of Absalom will have such a demoralizing effect on the troops who have just risked their lives to defend him against Absalom that he is throwing away everything which he has just regained. And it can hardly be accidental that it is only when he is old and feeble and a mere puppet in the hands of others that the succession to the throne can be settled by others who see, as he had never been able to do, the dangers into which the State has been thrown by his refusal to name a successor. So the author leaves us with yet another enigma: was it real greatness, or was it luck, together with the possession of loyal subordinates, which preserved David's kingdom and secured the all-important succession to the throne? It is significant that Joab, in the plainest speech in the book, emphasizes that David owes his life to his subordinates, and even comes close to suggesting that he owed his kingdom to them from the start (19.7).

It is in his portrayal of David's faults that the author comes closest to giving us an unambiguous picture. David's relations with his children provided an unusually good opportunity for a psychological study. The author never states baldly that the tragedies of Amnon, Absalom and Adonijah were due to David's own weaknesses, but he suggests it quite unmistakably in two ways: by portraying the sons as having inherited the weaknesses of their father and by describing in detail, quite objectively, the relations between David and *Absalom*.

The stories of the rape of Tamar and of Absalom's murder of Amnon show clearly how the sons had inherited the vices of their father. These stories immediately follow that of David's adultery, in which David had been guilty of criminal lust, treachery and murder. These crimes are now repeated by the sons, who are shown to have inherited both the passionate and the calculating sides of David's nature.

The author shows how David, far from taking firm measures to arrest the further effects of these inherited vices, displayed a total ineptitude in his treatment of both Amnon and Absalom. In saying that David was merely 'very angry' at Amnon's rape of Tamar, whereas Absalom 'hated' Amnon (13.21f.), he suggests that it was David's weakness which made Absalom take the law into his own hands. After the murder of Amnon it was again David's inability to take a decision in matters which concerned his own children (13.39-14.1) which led to further trouble. The notes of time—three years in exile in Geshur, 13.38; 'two full years' waiting in Jerusalem before being publicly reconciled with his father, 14.28—and the scene between Absalom and Joab in which Absalom speaks of his frustration (14.28-32) suggest the corrupting effect which David's inability to make up his mind had on Absalom; and the author then immediately (15.1-6) describes the inevitable result: the reconciliation comes too late, and so has the opposite effect from that intended by David, simply providing Absalom with an opportunity to prepare and carry out during the next four years (15.7) a plan of treason to which his father's folly had driven a young man whose original crime seems to have sprung from a noble desire to avenge a wicked deed against his sister.

The chapters which follow show that the real cause of David's vacillations was a maudlin sentimentality which overruled his common sense in all matters connected with his children. In the case of Amnon he had been ready to excuse one son for a heinous crime to the extent of wronging the other, who had avenged that crime. Now this same sentimentality was transferred to the second son, this time at the expense of the safety of the State. David, driven by Absalom's treason out of his own capital and made a fugitive in his own land, now has no thought but for the safety of the traitor: he orders Joab and the other commanders to 'deal gently' with him (18.5); his first question to each of the messengers who come to announce victory is not for the details of the battle or for the safety of his men, but for 'the young man Absalom' (18.29, 32); and in his grief at his death he shows that he cares for no one else (19.1-7). The picture of an obsessive love which brings death to its own objects and misery to the one who loves as well as to others can seldom have been surpassed even by modern novelists.

With characteristic restraint, the author did not judge it necessary to fill in the picture in detail either for *Amnon* or *Adonijah*. Apart from the significant comment in I Kings 1.6 that David never exercised any parental control over Adonijah, he leaves it to the reader to surmise that there was something amiss with the way in which David educated all his children, which could lead no less than three of them to such crimes as rape of a sister and treason against a father, and to violent deaths. In the case of Amnon, however, he gives us one more remarkable psychological insight: the 'sexual hatred'[40] which caused the lecher, after his desire was sated, to turn against the object of his lust, Tamar, so that 'the hatred with which he hated her was greater than the love with which he had loved her' (13.15).

The last of the sons of David named in the book—*Solomon*—can hardly be said to be more than a minor character, even if the whole of 1 Kings 1 and 2 is accepted as original. This reticence on the part of the author is easily understandable. If, as is probable, Solomon was the reigning king when the book was written, any psychological study of him, which would inevitably reveal his faults as well as his virtues, would be dangerous; and the author was hardly the man to spoil his work by concluding it with an insincere piece of flattery. Moreover, a full study of Solomon was hardly called for. His accession was the climax of the story, and a brief picture of Solomon sitting on the throne of his father was all that was needed to complete the work. The accounts of the fates of Adonijah, Abiathar, Joab and Shimei are no more than appendices which show that the author, like a Victorian novelist, felt that the artistic perfection of his work demanded the pulling together of all the strings in the final chapter, so that all suspense should be resolved.

Rost[41] characterizes the Solomon of these chapters as 'calculating and merciless'; but it may be doubted whether any real attempt is made by the author to depict his character. As with David, Solomon's motives are left in doubt, but in this case only because the portrait is not fully drawn. We do not know why he showed clemency towards Abiathar on the grounds of his past services to David when he had loyally shared his misfortunes (1 Kings 2.26), yet showed none towards Joab (2.28ff.), of whom the same could have been said.[42] Equally in the cases of Adonijah and Shimei, to whom Solomon offered a second chance (1.52f.; 2.36-38) but who were both eventually put to death on the grounds of further misbehaviour (2.13ff., 39ff.) no hint is given

[40] Cf. Hertzberg, p. 324.   [41] P. 231.
[42] II Sam. 19.7 is obviously a reference to the well known stories of David's and Joab's early careers.

which might enable the reader to decide whether Solomon's motives were sincere or whether he was indeed a 'calculating and merciless' man who intended from the first to remove these two men, but who for some unspecified reasons of policy needed an excuse. The only other glimpse of Solomon's character is given in 2.20ff., where he goes back on his promise to his mother that he will not refuse any request which she may make. Here, however, it is Bathsheba's stupidity rather than Solomon's unreliability which is emphasized.

Bathsheba, though also a minor character, is represented quite consistently and realistically in the three scenes in which she appears, as a rather negative person. On each occasion someone makes use of her: David for his lust (II Sam. 11), Nathan in order to defeat Adonijah's plot to seize the throne (I Kings 1) and Adonijah to further his romantic designs (I Kings 2). She is always a willing co-operator, never an initiator. On the second of these occasions she ought to have been aware of the threat to her own life and that of Solomon which was implicit in Adonijah's plot, but it was necessary for Nathan not only to persuade her of this (I Kings 1.12) but also to tell her how to use her influence over her aged husband, and how to bring him to the point of decision by alleging that he had already promised her to give the throne to Solomon (1.13, 17). After this we are not surprised to find her good-naturedly helping Adonijah in his romantic affairs (2.13ff.), without pausing to consider either whether there was some more sinister scheme behind them, or whether the whole plan was not more likely to send Adonijah to his funeral than to his wedding. We thus have a consistent and thoroughly credible picture of Bathsheba as a good-natured, rather stupid woman who was a natural prey both to more passionate and to cleverer men. We cannot know whether Bathsheba was still alive—and therefore queen-mother—when the book was written; but the author has suggested her character quite definitely, yet without committing himself directly.

Outside David's family, the most remarkable study of character in the book is that of *Joab*. His story, like that of Absalom, forms a substantial sub-plot second in importance only to that of David himself. He is depicted in a variety of situations which enable his complex character to take on flesh and blood; and we may note that this character is entirely consistent with that which emerges from the other stories about him in the earlier parts of Samuel, with which the author of the Succession Narrative and his readers will have been familiar.[43] Joab was already popularly known for his consistent loyalty to David and also for his capacity for committing sudden acts of murderous violence, carried out by treacherous means, when his honour or that of his family was injured (II Sam. 3.27-30). In the Succession Narrative these isolated traits of character are combined with others in a profound psychological study which, as in the case of David, gives the impression of a real person whose inconsistencies only reveal a complex nature.

By once again refraining from direct comment, the author leaves the reader free to speculate on Joab's motives in several incidents. We cannot exclude the possibility that he executed David's orders to kill Uriah (II Sam. 11.14-25) out of fear or anxiety to stand well with the king, or that his murder of Amasa (II Sam. 20.7-13) was done out of a spirit of personal spite against the man who had replaced him as commander-in-chief; or that his support of Adonijah was motivated by a calculation that his chances of retaining a position of power would be greater under Adonijah than under Solomon. But the overwhelming impression is that the chief motive for all his actions was loyalty. This loyalty, however, although mainly directed towards the person of the king, was not a blind unreasoning loyalty such as may have motivated Benaiah, the man who, ironically, was chosen to kill Joab (I Kings 2.34)—a subtle comment on the difference between David's men and the 'new men' of Solomon. Joab's loyalty throughout was above all a loyalty to Israel, whose security and greatness were his chief concern. To this Uriah, though innocent, must be sacrificed, because a public revelation of David's folly might endanger the safety of the State. Absalom, after his murder of Amnon, must be reconciled fully with David, because to leave him in an ambiguous situation was to court danger for the State. But when, as a result of David's continued weakness and hesitation, Absalom himself endangered the State by rebellion, Joab understood that not only must the rebellion be swiftly

---

[43] In the Succession Narrative there are a number of references and allusions to these other stories: in I Kings 2.5 David refers to Joab's murder of Abner (II Sam. 3.27), and his words 'What have I to do with you, you sons of Zeruiah?' (II Sam. 16.10; 19.22) recall II Sam. 3.39: 'These men the sons of Zeruiah are too hard for me.'

crushed, but its leader must be despatched without delay, in spite of David's express command (II Sam. 18.9-15). He was prepared to sacrifice not only the king's feelings, but also his own position and, it might be, his life, in the same service of the State.

In view of this clear consistency in Joab's motives, we may reasonably interpret Joab's murder of Amasa and his support of Adonijah's plot in a favourable sense: there is certainly no suggestion of disloyalty on his part in the murder of Amasa, and from our knowledge of Joab's former military success and reputation and the hasty and ill-considered nature of his replacement as commander-in-chief (II Sam. 19.13) we are entitled to believe that he regarded himself as the only man who could command the loyalty of the army and so crush Sheba's revolt. Here once again an innocent man—Amasa—and Joab's own safety are sacrificed for the good of the State: for there is no suggestion that Joab intended to use his military position against David. Finally we may well be led by the same reasoning to give credit to Joab for a sincere devotion to the State in his final recorded action, when he supported Adonijah against Solomon.

The moment which determined Joab's fate was that in which, in what must surely be some of the plainest words spoken by a loyal official to his king in the whole of ancient literature, Joab rebuked David to his face (II Sam. 19.1-8). In these words, spoken by Joab in private and under strong emotion, with an entire absence of the polite phrases which characterize the courtly speeches in the rest of the book, the author not only brings to life the ruggedness and forcefulness of Joab's character, but also reveals the complexity of his emotions and loyalties and of his relation to the king. The personal loyalty to David is rooted in the comradely sharing of past hardships ('all the evil that has come upon you from your youth until now') and in a genuine love between the two men: Joab speaks of himself and his companions as 'those who love you', and expects—and, it is implied, has always thought that he could count on—love in return. His most bitter accusation against David is that in his obsessive love for the traitor Absalom 'you have made it clear today that commanders and servants are nothing to you', and that 'you love those that hate you and hate those that love you'. Joab is not prepared to minimize his own part in the achievement and maintenance of David's greatness: he and his companions have 'saved David's life'. He cannot conceal his bitter disappointment at David's lack of gratitude and love.

This moment was crucial for Joab: it forced him, probably for the first time, to consider the nature of his loyalty. For the first time he saw that personal loyalty to David and loyalty to the State which he and David together had created were not necessarily identical; he is forced to choose between them, and he chooses the latter. For the first time he threatens to abandon his beloved leader: unless David will sacrifice his personal grief to the safety of the State, he will have no more to do with him.[44] The two stubborn old men who have spent their lives together have come to the parting of the ways. In forcing David to choose as he has chosen, and to trample on his most precious personal feelings, Joab seals his own fate.[45] This is one of the high points of tragedy in the book.

The author is not content to depict Joab as capable of only one emotion. Joab is not the simple, bluff soldier for whom loyalty alone is enough. Indeed, he exhibits statesmanlike qualities and shrewdness in the earlier scenes. He knows David's weaknesses, and is able to turn this knowledge to account, as when he uses the wise woman of Tekoa to play on his sensibilities. He is also prepared to use subtle means to defend himself, as in the carefully prepared message after the death of Uriah (II Sam. 11.18-25). But ultimately he is defeated by David's obsessive love for Absalom, which all his shrewdness is powerless to control; and in desperation he resorts to fatal, though effective, bluntness. The cause of Joab's tragedy lies not in any change in him, but in a deterioration in the character of David, who seems destined to destroy all whom he touches.

Several of the *minor characters*, although they appear on the scene only for brief moments, are, as von Rad remarked,[46] 'sharply outlined' and 'distinctively portrayed' in a few words. The main interest of *Ahithophel* and *Hushai* lies in their verbal skill; but the note about Ahithophel's suicide (II Sam. 17.23) gives some insight into his character: he is a professional coun-

---

[44] Cf. McKane's comment, p. 269: 'He has no time for a king who allows his private feelings to destroy his political judgment.'
[45] So B. Luther, *op. cit.*, p. 199; Auerbach, *op. cit.*, p. 248.
[46] 'Beginnings', p. 190.

sellor whose devotion to logical calculation is so much the dominating force in his life that he can apply it ruthlessly even to choosing the moment for his own death: he will not seek to prolong for a little while longer a life which he knows to be already forfeit; yet he will not die without setting his house in order. He is the 'new man', who is determined to be master of his own fate.

In the case of Hushai, the author raises a moral question which he leaves the reader to decide: can the gross deceit of giving deliberately false counsel in order to ruin Absalom, who trusted him, be justified by his motive, which was to serve the cause of his friend David? Is such a man to be considered as a loyal friend, or, on the contrary, a man totally lacking in moral principle? However we decide, we are left with the impression of a moral dilemma which faced a real person.

In *Ziba* and *Meribbaal* also we are confronted with an enigma, and one which David himself was unable to resolve; for having heard both their stories, he neither punished the one for slander nor the other for treason, but contented himself with settling the civil dispute by dividing the disputed property equally between them. Yet the author seems to convey, by subtle hints, the impression that it is Ziba who is the liar. It is he who cleverly takes advantage of David's confusion of mind during his flight from Jerusalem by alleging (II Sam. 16.3) that Meribbaal is plotting the restoration of the house of Saul—a scheme which David in a normal state of mind would recognize as quite incompatible with support of Absalom, but which was in fact the very thing of which David had always been afraid. The author shows his hand also by stating as a fact that Meribbaal had openly mourned for David throughout his absence (19.24). Although as elsewhere the author does not explicitly direct the reader's thoughts, he probably sought to portray Meribbaal as a colourless, well-meaning and rather ingenuous man who is tricked and betrayed by an unscrupulous servant who has fifteen sons to provide for (II Sam. 9.10) and who is placed from the beginning in a most advantageous position, free from proper supervision by a lame master who is forced to live away from his estates.

Of the other characters, some, like *Amasa* and the rebel *Sheba*, hardly come to life as individuals and are little more than parts of the historical scenery before which the lives of the major characters are enacted; *Shimei* too, though not lacking in positive qualities, is mainly used to illuminate the characters of David and Solomon. But even among the quite minor characters there are some who come to life through some characteristic trait, whether personal or typical: *Tamar*, who appears only in II Sam. 13, is no mere puppet but a spirited daughter of David, who tries to bring Amnon to his senses; her cousin *Jonadab* is the clever but irresponsible crony who shows Amnon how to achieve his criminal purpose but omits to point out the probable consequences if he succeeds in achieving it (II Sam. 13.5); the *wise woman of Tekoa* is a superb example of her class and profession; and finally *Benaiah*, Solomon's hatchet-man, who is sent to despatch first Adonijah, then Joab, and finally Shimei, and makes our blood curdle by the very impersonality of the account, is another character who remains an enigma: is he a man entirely without feelings, who would do anything to further his ambition—he succeeded his victim Joab as commander-in-chief (I Kings 2.35)— or was his ruthlessness the result of a blind and unquestioning loyalty to Solomon? This combination of a sharp delineation of a person's overt actions with an ambiguity about his motives, which we find in both major and minor characters, is one of the most convincing features of the story, because it corresponds to a problem which we encounter in real life.

(*e*) *Style*. As has already been suggested, much of the literary achievement of the Succession Narrative is due to mastery of style.[47] This is manifested both in the choice of individual words and expressions and in the broader aspects of movement and pace, contrast and irony.[48] Rost[49] pointed out how both narrative and dialogue are studded with vivid similes and comparisons, e.g. 'We are like water spilt on the ground', II Sam. 14.14; 'The counsel which Ahithophel gave was as if one consulted the oracle of God', 16.23; 'as a bride comes home to her husband', 17.3; 'you are worth ten thousand of us', 18.3; 'they are enraged, like a bear robbed of her cubs', 17.8. He noted the entire absence of such expressions in, for example, the more formal Ark narra-

---

[47] The most detailed study of this is that of Rost, pp. 218-226.
[48] Cf. S. R. Driver, *op. cit.*, p. 183: 'The style is singularly bright, flowing and picturesque.'
[49] P. 220.

tive in the earlier part of Samuel. He also drew attention to the author's use of contrast. This may be verbal, as when Meribbaal, after referring to himself self-deprecatingly as a 'dead dog' (II Sam. 9.8) is thereupon honoured as a 'king's son' (9.11), or it may be a contrast of character, as when Shimei's rage and hatred is contrasted with David's calm and magnanimity (16.5-14), or the son's treachery with the foreigner's loyalty (15.13-22).

The way in which the author varies, sometimes quite dramatically, the speed of the narrative in order to create, and then release, tension and suspense, has been noted by a number of writers. B. Luther[50] drew attention to the way in which, in II Sam. 11f., the reader is deliberately kept in suspense: the story of David's adultery is followed not by an account of his punishment but by a note of Bathsheba's pregnancy (11.5). Again, after the swiftly told murder of Uriah, there is a further delay (11.26-27a) before retribution comes in the person of Nathan. Rost[51] gave another example: the way in which, immediately after David's dramatic flight from the city, the author lingers almost unbearably (15.18-16.14) over his departure when the reader is anxious to know what happened next. The departure scene is deliberately made more ponderous by the frequent repetition of the verb 'pass on' ('*ābar*, 11 times). Finally, von Rad pointed out how in II Sam. 18.19ff. 'the narrator heightens the tension by relating at length how the young and unsuspecting Ahimaaz is eager to carry tidings of the victory to the king'.[52]

These deliberate delays, to which we should add the occasions when the author postpones a sequel even longer, as in the story of Meribbaal and Ziba, build up a tension which is then often suddenly released in a rapidly told conclusion which leaves the reader breathless: a fateful deed is done (II Sam. 11.4; 13.14), a kingdom lost (15.13-16) or a murder committed (20.9f.) in a flash. The rapidity with which an action can be carried out which will have lifelong consequences is conveyed to the reader by the use—a rarity with this writer—of the simplest form of Hebrew prose construction: a succinct series of consecutive verbs.

The opposite of suspense is dramatic irony, when the reader is entertained by knowing in advance what will happen, and so able to watch the characters playing their parts in ignorance of their fate. In a sense the whole book is an extended example of

[50] *Op. cit.*, pp. 189f.   [51] P. 218.   [52] 'Beginnings', p. 186.

dramatic irony, for the reader already knows how the succession was settled and what was in store for the main characters. But the sense of irony is frequently heightened both by hints to the reader of what is to come, of which some examples have already been given, and by more concrete touches: David's ignorance of the real meaning of Nathan's parable and of the wise woman of Tekoa's story; his encouragement of Tamar's visit to her supposedly sick brother Amnon (II Sam. 13.7); his permission to Absalom to invite the king's sons to the fateful feast (13.23-27); the false rumour that all the king's sons have been killed (13.30f.); David's blessing on Absalom's visit to Hebron, supposedly to pay his vow (15.7-9); his impatience to know the result of the battle (18.24ff.); Adonijah's feasting, in ignorance of Solomon's proclamation as king (I Kings 1.41).

From the above study it will be apparent that the praise accorded to the author of the Succession Narrative as a literary genius far superior to his predecessors is fully justified, and that the book is worthy to be compared in all important respects with a modern novel. Whether this unexpected leap forward in the art of Hebrew narrative is due entirely to the genius of the author, building upon earlier native attempts in the genre, or whether he was influenced by the new insights into human character and the nature of human society which had flooded into Israel during his own generation from more sophisticated civilizations, will be examined in the chapters which follow.

But in arriving at the conclusion that the work is a novel —albeit a historical novel—rather than a work of history properly speaking, we are still some way from a full understanding of its character and purpose. No doubt purely literary and artistic aims and the desire to entertain the reader occupied an important place in the author's mind. But it is extremely unlikely that these were his only, or even his main, aims. He would not have chosen so recent a period of history as the setting for his story if he had not some other, more practical, purpose. We are therefore driven to an examination of other possibilities.

3. *The Succession Narrative as a national epic*

A number of writers[53] have thought of the book as a national

[53] Pfeiffer, *op. cit.*, pp. 357f.; Jacob, *art. cit.*, p. 29; North, *op. cit.*, p. 34;

epic,[54] motivated by pride in the nation's achievements and a desire to record, not necessarily with scrupulous regard for strict historical accuracy but rather poetically, the most glorious and significant chapter in Israel's history. At first sight, there might seem to be much to support this theory. We must, of course, assume that David's earlier achievements were already known and recorded. Now in the Succession Narrative David is seen as crowning these achievements by putting down internal rebellions which threatened the new empire and finally handing on his throne to Solomon, so securing the stability of the dynasty. Seen from the point of view of patriotic Israelites living in the reign of Solomon, this work would be the final chapter in the national epic which told of the rise of Israel to greatness.

But there are two considerations which render this interpretation improbable. The first is the treatment of the principal characters, especially David. On any interpretation of the period, David was the chief architect of Israel's greatness, and a national epic which did not represent him as a splendid hero would be inconceivable. It is quite impossible to believe that if the author's main intention was to sing the glories of the reign he would have gone out of his way, as he appears to have done, to emphasize that David was not only a murderer and adulterer but also a man who had brought the nation to the brink of disaster by sacrificing its security to his personal feelings. The argument that David is presented, in spite of his faults, basically as a sympathetic character is hardly to the point here: it is admiration, not sympathy for the hero which is required in an epic; and we only have to compare the stories about David in the earlier parts of the Books of Samuel with the Succession Narrative to see how far the stature of David as a hero has been reduced in the latter.

This refusal to make David into a hero is not to be accounted for, as in some other Old Testament narratives, by a feeling that it is Yahweh who ought to be the true hero: the author's view of the hidden nature of God's guidance of history does not allow him to bring Yahweh into prominence in this way. There is, in fact, no hero in the Succession Narrative. It is true that the author believed that it was through David that God's will was

McKane, *op. cit.*, p. 19; Lods, *op. cit.*, p. 165; A. Bentzen, *Introduction to the Old Testament* II, Copenhagen, 1948, p. 95.

[54] Or as *part* of a national epic.

being fulfilled, and gave expression to this belief in a few passages in which David expresses his sense of being in God's hands (II Sam. 12.16-23; 15.19f., 25, 31; 16.10-12); but this neither makes him a hero, nor does it make the work into an epic. The impression of David which is left with the reader is of a man who, whether by luck or providence, survived the consequences of his own blundering and folly to end his days in the enjoyment of a success and achievement which he did not deserve. Whatever the moral or religious lesson to be learned, the character of David, which dominates the entire narrative, is hardly the basis for a national epic, whether religious or secular.

Neither is the treatment of Absalom consistent with a theory of national epic. There is no room in such a work for a partly sympathetic portrayal of a man who, whatever excuse he may have had for his actions, brought nothing but evil upon the nation. The difference between the Succession Narrative and a national epic becomes apparent if we compare it with the portrait of David in Chronicles, which has a much better claim to be called a religious national epic. The Chronicler entirely passed over the faults of David as being incompatible with his purpose, and showed no sympathetic interest in the other figures of the period.

A second consideration which makes the theory of national epic improbable is the limited range of the material included in the Succession Narrative. It is exclusively concerned with David's family and his court; and the author has evidently passed over events which would have been suitable for inclusion in a national epic, while including much which is not.

Undoubtedly the achievements of David must have kindled a strong sense of national pride among the Israelites of his time, and the successful handing on of the kingdom to Solomon without loss will have been seen as the event which set the seal to those achievements and assured their permanence. But the complex and often unsavoury story of how this came about which we have in the Succession Narrative, far from adding an epic quality to these achievements, would rather detract from their impressiveness.

4. *The Succession Narrative as a moral or religious tale*

An Old Testament narrative which carried no moral or religious lesson whatever would be most unusual, and only a few writers have judged the Succession Narrative to be wholly secular in character.[55] On the other hand, it is generally agreed that its religious or theological point of view is far less easy to define than is the case with most Old Testament narratives, where God is specifically represented as intervening directly in human affairs through dreams and visions, prophetic oracles, theophanies and visitations of sudden death.[56] The views of Jacob[57] and B. Luther[58] that the characters are 'types' or 'models' of human behaviour intended to convey moral warnings, and of Morton Smith[59] that the work is fundamentally a moral tract, while not entirely wide of the mark, do not do justice to the author's subtle understanding of human nature or to his literary skill. Simple moral or religious exhortation does not conceal itself behind psychological complexities: to be effective, it must present its message in terms of black and white and point its moral explicitly.

This is not to say that the Succession Narrative is devoid of moral or religious teaching. On the contrary, it will be argued in a later chapter[60] that the author had a strong educational motive, and that he also expressed a particular point of view. But to concede this no more solves the problem of the main purpose of the work than does the discovery that it is a novel. The question why the author chose to recount the events which led to Solomon's accession to the throne rather than some other story still remains unanswered.

5. *The Succession Narrative as political propaganda*

In looking for a precise motive for the composition of the Succession Narrative it is important to bear in mind that it is entirely concerned with dynastic politics. The author's own loyalty to the Davidic dynasty is not in doubt. Although he did

---

[55] E.g. E. Meyer, *Geschichte des Altertums*, vol. 2, 3rd edn, 1953, pp. 285f. (quoted by von Rad, 'Beginnings', p. 197): 'purely secular'; 'any kind of religious colouring is excluded'; Lods, *op. cit.*, p. 164: 'there is no question of an edifying intention . . .; no prominence whatever is given to the divine activity.'

[56] The only passage in the Succession Narrative where such things occur is the story of Nathan's parable and the death of the child in II Sam. 12.1-15. It is for this reason that some writers have considered this entire passage to be an interpolation.

[57] *Art. cit.*, p. 30.

[58] *Op. cit.*, p. 193.

[59] *Art. cit.*, pp. 167-169.

[60] Ch. 3, *infra*.

not hesitate to make an extremely critical estimate of David both as a man and as king, and although it was not his intention to compose an epic with David as its hero, he nevertheless clearly shared the sentiments which he frequently put into the mouths of his characters, concerning the divine approval of the Davidic dynasty. These testify to a belief in a special relationship between David and his God. They refer to Yahweh as 'David's God' (II Sam. 14.17; 18.28; I Kings 1.17); and Benaiah expresses a general belief when he says that Yahweh has 'been with my lord the king' throughout his life (I Kings 1.37). David himself swears by Yahweh, 'who has redeemed my life from adversity' (I Kings 1.29).[61]

This conviction that David, with all his faults, was and remained throughout his life the king appointed by Yahweh extended also, as the 'foundation document' of II Sam. 7 also shows, to David's legitimate descendants. It is evident from David's prayer of thanksgiving for the granting of a successor in I Kings 1.48, and even from the deceitful words of Hushai to Absalom in II Sam. 16.19—'Whom should I serve? Should it not be his son? As I have served your father, so I will serve you'—that the dynastic theology expounded in II Sam. 7 had already been widely accepted when the Succession Narrative was written.[62]

It is equally clear that the author believed that Solomon, the *de facto* successor of David, was also the successor designated by both Yahweh and David. This belief is expressed in the words of David in I Kings 1.48—'Blessed be Yahweh, the God of Israel, who has granted one of my offspring to sit on my throne this day'—and in I Kings 1.35—'He shall be king in my stead; and I have appointed him to be ruler over Israel and over Judah'. It is also expressed by Benaiah in I Kings 1.37: 'As Yahweh has been with my lord the king, even so may he be with Solomon, and make his throne greater than the throne of my lord King David'. These words of Benaiah, coming so emphatically at the climax of the whole book, have a good claim to be considered the key to the problem of the purpose for which the book was written: the story of the succession to the throne has been told

[61] Cf. Rost, p. 235.
[62] See M. Noth, 'David and Israel in II Samuel VII' (*The Laws in the Pentateuch*, Edinburgh, 1966, pp. 250-259; translated from *Mélanges bibliques rédigés en l'honneur de André Robert*, Paris, 1957, pp. 122-130) on the early date of II Sam. 7.

in order to justify Solomon's claim to be the true king of Israel, and to strengthen the régime against its critics.

That Benaiah's sentiments exactly express the view of the author is confirmed above all by his own statement concerning Solomon in II Sam. 12.24b-25, that 'Yahweh loved him, and sent a message by Nathan the prophet; so he called his name Jedidiah, because of Yahweh'—a statement which is significantly placed immediately before the series of incidents which excluded Solomon's half-brothers from the throne.[63] The stories concerning the unsuccessful candidates are thus framed between the implied divine promise concerning Solomon and the fulfilment of that promise.

As has already been pointed out,[64] the personal character of Solomon is not fully portrayed in the book; but there is no reason to suppose that the little which is said about him is intended to be critical. It is perhaps significant that no mention is made of him at all between the notice of his birth and naming (II Sam. 12.24f.) and the story of his enthronement (from I Kings 1.10). He thus remains an unknown, mysterious figure during the period when his brothers are attempting to usurp the throne. This impersonal treatment is perhaps intended to emphasize that he stood aloof from the conflict. Absalom's and Adonijah's plots stand condemned as arrogant attempts to snatch the kingdom by force; but the rightful heir, through none of his own seeking— for there is no suggestion that he had any part in the intrigue of Nathan and Bathsheba related in I Kings 1.11ff.—is carried by the events themselves to his appointed destiny.

The failure of the author to paint a glowing picture of Solomon may possibly—though we cannot be sure of this—indicate that he had no great enthusiasm for him as a man; but the whole tenor of the book shows that he had complete confidence in the dynasty as divinely appointed, and in the rightness of Solomon's claim to the throne. This is the real purpose of the stories of Amnon and Absalom: to show that 'neither the man of unbridled sensuality nor the fratricide and usurper . . . are acceptable kings.'[65]

[63] Hertzberg, p. 377.
[64] Pp. 39f., *supra*.
[65] Hertzberg, *loc. cit.*; cf. also Weiser, *op. cit.*, p. 165. Hertzberg notes that by these criteria David himself was equally unworthy, but—though this may seem to be a flaw in the book, where the author's psychological interests have been allowed to predominate over the main theme—it is evident that

The fact that the author thus wrote, as Rost put it,[66] '*ad majorem gloriam Salomonis*', but in a dynastic rather than a personal sense, suggests the existence of some particular political circumstances which inspired or necessitated the writing of the book. Nothing else could adequately account for the tremendous insistence, especially in the closing chapters, on the legitimacy of Solomon's accession. Although the author, no sycophant, had no interest in writing a fulsome eulogy of Solomon, he was deeply concerned about the stability of the dynasty and régime. The insistence on the unworthiness of the other candidates and on the correctness of Solomon's appointment, anointing and enthronement strongly suggests that the book was written at a time when the stability and legitimacy of the régime were being threatened.

Vriezen, who came to this conclusion,[67] pointed out that there were two periods in Solomon's reign when such dangers existed: the first and the last years of the reign. With regard to the first of these periods, I Kings 1 and 2 leave no doubt that several years elapsed (2.1, 39) before 'the kingdom was established in the hand of Solomon' (2.46b), and although the author writes as if this had now been fully accomplished, this attitude of confident assurance may well have been adopted with the intention of discouraging disaffected elements which in fact still continued to cherish hopes of overthrowing Solomon. The cause of Adonijah, supported as it had been by such men as Joab and Abiathar, probably attracted considerable sympathy, and the harsh treatment meted out to Adonijah and his two supporters, who, after David, were the best known and the most beloved of all the nation's leaders, would be likely at first to have kindled rather than to have extinguished a feeling of sympathy for them which may well have lasted for some while longer. All this would naturally have been concealed by the author of the Succession Narrative.[68]

the special grace accorded to David was regarded by his contemporaries as something altogether exceptional.

[66] P. 234.

[67] *De Compositie van de Samuël-Boeken* (*Orientalia Neerlandica*), Leiden, 1948, pp. 167-189.

[68] The fact that there is no mention of such disaffection at the beginning of the account of Solomon's reign in I Kings 3 is no proof that there was none. In the account of Solomon's reign, all the references to discontent and rebellion have been relegated to the final chapter (11.14-40) for schematic

This dating is by far the most probable. It provides an entirely satisfactory explanation of the character of the Succession Narrative as a work written to rally support for the régime by legitimizing Solomon's position; and it also accounts for the 'testament of David' at the end of the book as intended to justify the executions of Joab (I Kings 2.5f.) and of the last remaining Benjamite leader, Shimei (I Kings 2.8f.) as duties laid upon Solomon by the dying David. That the Succession Narrative is not the only example of such a propagandist narrative will be shown in a later chapter.[69]

Vriezen's second suggestion, that the book might have been written during the last years of Solomon's reign, is much less probable. It is true that those years also were years of political unrest and disaffection, as is shown by the account of Jeroboam's revolt and flight to Egypt (I Kings 11.26f., 40),[70] and by the rebellion of the north which immediately followed Solomon's death. But by that time a work of propaganda which dealt only with events before Solomon's accession and made no mention of the events of his reign would hardly be effective; and if the late date were accepted we should also be forced to abandon the well-nigh universally held and extremely probable view that the book was written by a man who had been personally acquainted with David and his court, since it is unlikely that he would have still been active so long afterwards.[71]

We may therefore suggest with some confidence that the Succession Narrative was written during the early years of Solomon's reign, soon after the events described in I Kings 2, and while

rather than chronological reasons. In fact, I Kings 11.21, 25 specifically state that the revolts in the provinces of the empire there mentioned occurred at the beginning, not the end of the reign. See Eissfeldt, *Introduction*, p. 288.

[69] Ch. 4, *infra*.

[70] If the statement that Jeroboam fled to Shishak king of Egypt (I Kings 11.40) is correct, his rebellion must have taken place after 935, when Solomon had been on the throne for about 26 years and about 13 years before his death (see J. Bright, *A History of Israel*, London, 1960, p. 208 and n. 105).

[71] Rost (p. 234) also put the date of composition in the early years of Solomon's reign, although his reason—that the book contains no hint that the author knew of the later troubles of the reign—is based on the opinion that the book reflects an atmosphere of political optimism and confidence rather than one of political instability. However, his argument (p. 233) that the book must in any case have been written before Solomon's death, because it shows no knowledge of the division of the kingdom, is a valid one. For the author, the 'kingdom' is undoubtedly the undivided empire which David had built.

the régime was still threatened by disaffected parties: it is primarily a political document intended to support the régime by demonstrating its legitimacy and justifying its policies. At the same time it is a work of great literary distinction and independence, far from being a political hack-work commissioned by the king. It was written by a member of a sophisticated and cultured court circle, who combined literary skill and great psychological insight with a new understanding of the working of Yahweh in history and with a deep devotion to the house of David as the principal instrument through which he guided the destinies of his Chosen People.[72]

[72] Although I believe that it is possible to define the cultural and professional circle to which the author belonged, there seems to be no point in attempting, as has often been done in the past, to identify him with one of the persons named in the book.

III

WISDOM IN THE SUCCESSION NARRATIVE

THE political motive proposed in the foregoing chapter accounts for much of the contents of the Succession Narrative. But it is hardly sufficient to account for its literary character or its psychological interests. For this we must return to a more detailed consideration of the milieu in which the author lived.

As has already been stated,[1] the interests of the men who surrounded David and Solomon were not confined to politics. These men constituted the cultural elite of the nation, and the educational system by which they had been trained prepared its pupils not merely for a professional career but for the enjoyment of life in all its aspects, making no distinction between the ethical, social, political and cultural, but regarding them all as comprised within the single notion of the 'good' (*ṭōb*). Its discipline (*mūsār*) was directed towards the achievement of success and prosperity through the acquisition of 'wisdom' (*ḥokmā*), which conferred on its possessors the gift of 'life' (*ḥayyīm*), the sum of all human success, prosperity and happiness.

A. THE SUCCESSION NARRATIVE AND THE BOOK OF PROVERBS: A GENERAL COMPARISON

Our main source of information about this educational and scribal ideal is the Book of Proverbs,[2] which contains teaching given in the scribal schools. A comparison of the teaching of Proverbs with the Succession Narrative may therefore be expected to shed some light on the cultural milieu of the latter.[3]

[1] Pp. 4ff., *supra*.
[2] See p. 6, n. 13, *supra*.
[3] A possible connexion between the Succession Narrative and the wisdom circles has already been tentatively suggested by some writers: Duesberg, *op. cit.*, pp. 333-338; Noth, 'Bewährung', p. 236; von Rad, *Theology* I, p. 56; H. H. Guthrie, *God and History in the Old Testament*, London, 1961, p. 119; R. A. Carlson, *David the Chosen King*, Stockholm, 1964, pp. 137, 147.

1. *The importance of 'counsel'*[4]

Great prominence is given in the Succession Narrative to wisdom (*ḥokmā*) and its practical expression in 'counsel' (*'ēṣā*) as accomplishments necessary to the successful conduct of both public and private affairs. As political acumen, wisdom is regarded as a highly desirable, if not essential, quality in kings: in II Sam. 14.20 the woman of Tekoa expresses the popular view that the king 'has wisdom like the wisdom of the angel of God to know all things that are on the earth', and in I Kings 2.6, 9 we see how this wisdom is translated into ruthless political action. David in his final instructions to Solomon urges him to show his wisdom by putting to death Joab and Shimei as potential dangers to the throne: 'Act therefore according to your wisdom, and do not let his head go down to Sheol in peace'; 'Now therefore hold him not guiltless, for you are a wise man; you will know what you ought to do to him, and you shall bring his head down with blood to the grave.' This is royal 'wisdom.'

But in practice kings rarely acted without the advice (*'ēṣā*) of men who were recognized as professional counsellors: Ahithophel is specifically called 'David's counsellor' (*yō'ēṣ*, II Sam. 15.12), and in II Sam. 16.20-17.14 we are given a most valuable detailed account of a royal council meeting at which such men were consulted. Absalom, as king, presides and invites two counsellors to give their advice: 'Give your counsel; what shall we do?' When each has spoken, the assembly decides between them: 'The counsel of Hushai is better than the counsel of Ahithophel.' The decision is then put into effect: counsel is translated into action. Although this incident took place at the court of the usurper Absalom, there is every reason to suppose that this was the normal form of the council meetings held by David himself: Ahithophel is represented as performing his usual role of 'king's counsellor', and the author is drawing on his own knowledge of court procedure.

Such counsel could have an authority far greater than that of mere opinion: the authority of Ahithophel's counsel is placed on the same level as that of the word of God (II Sam. 16.23); and David's first thought when he learns that Ahithophel has joined

---

[4] On counsel and counsellors in Israel see P. A. H. de Boer, 'The Counsellor', VT Suppl. 3, 1955, pp. 42-71.

the rebels is to pray to Yahweh that he will intervene to nullify his counsel (II Sam. 15.31). That in the event his counsel was rejected in favour of that of Hushai is attributed by the author to the action of Yahweh upon the minds of the assembly (II Sam. 17.14b).

Counsel was not confined to the royal council-chamber: Nathan (I Kings 1.12) offers to Bathsheba, in private, counsel whose purpose is to persuade her to influence the king through personal persuasion, and so to bring about political action which will secure her own safety and position and that of her son.

Nor were wisdom and council confined to public life. The wits which had been sharpened, and the skills which had been acquired, through the scribal education could be made to serve private as well as public ends, whether good or evil. The fact that Jonadab, David's nephew, who counselled his friend Amnon how to seduce Tamar (II Sam. 13.3-5), is described as 'very wise' (*ḥākām meʿōd*) shows that 'wisdom' is a purely intellectual and morally neutral quality. It can even be found among those who have received no special training, such as—presumably— the two 'wise women' who appear in II Sam. 14.2ff. and 20.16ff.; but the wisdom depicted by the author of the Succession Narrative is mainly the politically oriented wisdom of the trained official, or of the king.

The examples given above are all of passages in which the words *ḥākām, ʿēṣā* or their cognates occur, and they give some indication of the role played by these concepts in Israelite political and court life as depicted in the Succession Narrative. But a full appreciation of the extent to which they dominate the thought of the author can only be obtained from an examination of the other incidents in the story. It then becomes apparent that, even when these words themselves are not used, wisdom and counsel are present as fundamental concepts throughout the book. Every incident illustrates either the application of wisdom and/or counsel to a particular situation, or the consequences of not applying it: the folly of acting without it. The most obvious cases of acting without wisdom are David's adultery, Amnon's rape of Tamar, and Adonijah's request, when he was already in an exceedingly precarious position, for the hand of Abishag. The consequences in each case were disastrous. But in almost every other incident in the book the characters act only after they have calculated their chances of success and the probable consequences; and this calculation takes the form either of solitary reflexion, in which—even though the word may not occur—the person in question may be said to be acting 'according to his wisdom' (the phrase occurs in I Kings 2.6) or of counsel given by one person to another. The following examples, out of many, will illustrate this point: David, after his preliminary act of folly, tries to extricate himself from his predicament by acts of 'wisdom' (II Sam. 11.14-25); Amnon receives counsel from Jonadab which leads him to the rape of Tamar—though in this case the counsel is bad counsel, and therefore in fact folly, because it concerns itself only with methods and fails to calculate the consequences. The story in II Sam. 14 of Joab's use of the woman of Tekoa is really a story of Joab's wisdom rather than that of the woman: Joab applied his wisdom 'in order to change the course of affairs' (v. 20). Absalom's actions by which he 'stole the hearts of the men of Israel' (II Sam. 15.1-6) are also an example of calculating wisdom; so also is David's action in sending Hushai to give false counsel to Absalom (15.33-35), and again in sending the priests back to Jerusalem to act as spies (15.27f., 35f.). Joab's advice to David in II Sam. 19.5-7 is an excellent example of the role of the state counsellor, although the word itself is not used.

A few quotations from Proverbs will be sufficient to show that this world of the Succession Narrative, with its political intrigue and its high regard for wisdom and counsel, is precisely the same as that of the wisdom literature.[5]

On the general necessity of taking thought before acting:

In everything a prudent man ('*ārūm*) acts with knowledge,
But a fool parades his folly. (Prov. 13.16)[6]

The wise of heart (*ḥᵃkam-lēb*) is called a man of discernment.
(16.21a)

A prudent man sees danger and hides himself;
But the simple go on, and pay for it. (27.12)

[5] It should be noted that the vocabulary of Proverbs is rich in synonyms, and that various words are used—e.g. '*ārūm*, 'prudent'; *sōd*, 'counsel'— which are virtually synonymous with *ḥākām*, '*ēṣā*, etc.

[6] On the textual problems of the quotations from Proverbs in this chapter, modern commentaries should be consulted. Justification of the translations will be given in the notes only where the general sense is seriously disputed.

On the necessity and effectiveness of counsel:

> Plans are established by counsel;
> By wise guidance wage your war. (20.18)

Some proverbs clearly refer to the royal council-meeting which we have seen in operation in the Succession Narrative, with consultation of more than one counsellor, followed by the decision of the assembly:

> Without counsel (*sōd*) plans go wrong,
> But with many counsellors (*yō'ᵃṣīm*) they succeed. (15.22)

> By wise guidance you can wage war,
> And victory comes from an abundance of counsellors. (24.6)

Proverbs also knows of wicked counsellors, like Jonadab:

> A man of violence entices his friend,
> And leads him into a way which is not good. (16.29)

> Like the glaze covering an earthen vessel
> Are smooth lips with an evil heart. (26.23)

Such proverbs as these may refer to human situations in general; but what is expressed in general terms is often repeated with specific reference to the king and those who surround him:

> Righteous lips are the delight of a king,
> And he loves him who speaks what is right. (16.13)

> Take away the wicked from the presence of a king,
> And his throne will be established in righteousness. (25.5)

> If a ruler listens to falsehood,
> All his officials will be wicked. (29.12)

Such references to the king make it clear that these proverbs are not intended primarily for everyman, but were written for those who came into daily contact with the king, in order to guide them in both their public and private lives. In other words, they reflect the same milieu and express the same concerns as the Succession Narrative.

2. *Retribution*

In spite of the great importance which they attach to human wisdom, both books recognize that the sphere of its efficacy is limited. No amount of shrewdness can enable the wicked man to avoid the inevitable consequences of his wickedness. This is a commonplace repeated many times in Proverbs; one example will suffice:

> Misfortune pursues sinners,
> But prosperity rewards the righteous. (13.21)

With regard to the Succession Narrative, von Rad's remark that 'the motive of retribution . . . pervades the whole work'[7] is illustrated in scene after scene; indeed the whole book from II Sam. 11 onwards might be described as 'David's sin and its consequences'.[8]

The fact that most of the statements in Proverbs on this subject are quite general, and give no indication of the means by which retribution will overtake the wicked suggests that the author, who is here commenting on his own experience of life, intends it to be understood that retribution will come, not by a miraculous divine intervention, but through natural means—a further point at which Proverbs is at one with the Succession Narrative, as we shall see. Some proverbs, however, add a further refinement to the doctrine of retribution through natural means: it will come as the unexpected but direct result of the evil action itself, so bringing on the sinner a fate which is uniquely appropriate to his deed: the violent will suffer violence and the trickster will be tricked:

> The violence of the wicked will sweep them away. (21.7a)

> He who digs a pit will fall into it,
> And a stone will come back upon him who sets it rolling.
> (26.27)

This principle is also exemplified in the Succession Narrative. The most obvious example is the prophecy of Nathan (II Sam. 12.11f.) which is fulfilled in 16.22: the humiliation of David through the dishonouring of his concubines by Absalom is seen as a fitting punishment for his humiliation of Uriah in taking his wife. The point of these verses, which may be an interpolation, is made more subtly in other ways: David is punished for his adultery by seeing Amnon rush to his ruin through an uncontrolled passion similar to his own; he is punished for the murder

---

[7] 'Beginnings', p. 196.   [8] See p. 23, n. 28, *supra*.

of Uriah by seeing Absalom brought to ruin and death as the result of a train of circumstances which also began with murder; Absalom, who lifted himself up in rebellion, dies 'between heaven and earth' (II Sam. 18.9), having been caught by his hair, which was the symbol of his pride and arrogance (14.25 27)[9]; Joab the man of violence comes to a violent death. Other examples could be given.

3. *Yahweh as the controller of human destiny*

In Proverbs, side by side with the numerous statements about retribution which suggest the working of an impersonal nemesis, there stand others which plainly state that it is Yahweh who controls human destiny in accordance with his own purpose:

> The eyes of Yahweh are in every place,
> Keeping watch over the evil and the good. (15.3)

> A man's mind plans his way,
> But Yahweh directs his steps. (16.9)

> Many are the plans in the mind of a man,
> But it is the purpose of Yahweh which will be established.
> (19.21)

> A man's steps are ordered by Yahweh;
> How then can man understand his way? (20.24)

These passages, which occur in the same sections of Proverbs as those previously quoted, are not to be thought of as corrections made at a later time by a pious Yahwist to an older, more secular type of wisdom.[10] Both types of proverb are also found side by side in non-Israelite books: Proverbs is in this respect representative of wisdom teaching as a whole. The Egyptian *Wisdom of Amen-em-opet*[11] is a good example. Here we find examples of the impersonal operation of retribution, e.g.

> If thou spend thy life-time with these things in thy heart,
> Thou wilt find it a success. (*Amen-em-opet*, ch. I, col. 3, lines 17f.)

[9] Cf. McKane, *op. cit.*, *ad loc.*
[10] For this view, no longer generally held, see e.g. Pfeiffer, *Introduction*, pp. 649ff.
[11] Full translation in F. Ll. Griffith, 'The Teaching of Amenophis, the son of Kanekht', *JEA* 12, 1926, pp. 191-231. J. A. Wilson in *ANET*, pp. 421-424, and J. M. Plumley in D. W. Thomas, *Documents from Old Testament Times*, pp. 172-186, have only translated selections from the work.

Covet not the property of a dependent,
Nor hunger for his bread.
Verily the property of a dependent is a choking for the throat,
It is a vomiting for the gullet. (*Ibid.*, XI, 14 5-8)

But more frequently *Amen-em-opet* speaks of human destiny as controlled by an all-seeing, all-powerful God; and this teaching is often expressed in terms very similar to those used in Proverbs:

The Ape (i.e. the god Thoth) dwelleth in the house of Khmûn,
But his eye travels round the Two Lands;
If he sees him that perverts with his finger,
He takes away his provisions in the deep waters.
(*Ibid.*, XV, 17.9-12)
Man knoweth not how the morrow will be;
The events of the morrow are in the hand of God.
God is ever in his success,
Man is ever in his failure.
The words which men say are one thing,
The things which God doeth are another.
(*Ibid.*, XVIII, 19.13-17)
The tongue of a man is the rudder of the boat,
But the Universal Lord is its pilot. (*Ibid.*, XVIII, 20.5f.)

Verily thou knowest not the designs of God,
Thou canst not realize the morrow. (*Ibid.*, XXI, 22.5f.)

We can only conclude that in both Proverbs and Egyptian wisdom literature these two types of statement express two complementary aspects of wisdom thought: the impersonal statements emphasize the natural and non-miraculous character of the process of retribution, while the others express the conviction that human destiny nevertheless comes within the sphere of God's control. There is tension here, but not contradiction.

A similar tension seems to have existed in the mind of the author of the Succession Narrative: he believed that a man's evil deeds lead, by a natural process, to their own evil consequences; but he also believed in the working of a divine providence which is beyond man's understanding: the establishment of the Davidic dynasty in the hands of Solomon was an event which hardly seemed to correspond to David's deserts, and could only be put down to the fulfilment of Yahweh's mysterious purpose.[12] It

[12] For a fuller discussion of this view of Yahweh's activity see especially von Rad, 'Beginnings', pp. 195ff.; *Theology* I, pp. 51ff.; 313ff.

was in accordance with the former of these beliefs that he refrained almost entirely from direct comment on the events of his story: the destiny of the characters must be seen to be working itself out naturally and in accordance with the normal process of retribution. But it was the latter belief that led him on three—but only three—significant occasions to draw the reader's attention by direct comment to the operation of Yahweh's mysterious purpose—though even here, operating through natural means—concerning the dynasty[13]:

But the thing which David had done displeased Yahweh. (II Sam. 11.27)

She bore a son, and he called his name Solomon. And Yahweh loved him. (12.24)

For Yahweh had ordained to defeat the good counsel of Ahithophel, so that Yahweh might bring evil upon Absalom. (17.14)

These comments are concerned, not with the operation of retribution in the lives of the characters, but with the hidden purpose of Yahweh with regard to the succession: his displeasure in 11.27 led to the death, and so to the elimination as a candidate for the throne, of the first son of David and Bathsheba; 12.24 confirms, from the moment of his birth, the destiny of Solomon; and 17.14, interjected at the moment of David's greatest danger, sounds the death knell of the usurper Absalom. Their tenor corresponds exactly to the teaching of the proverbs which we have quoted above, which speak of Yahweh's universal knowledge of human designs and of his hidden purpose which frustrates men's plans. Indeed, the third (17.14) echoes Prov. 16.9; 19.21 with absolute precision.

II Samuel 17.14 also illustrates another fundamental principle of Proverbs, about counsel. It is intended to be understood as the answer to David's prayer in 15.31: 'Yahweh, I pray thee, turn the counsel of Ahithophel into foolishness.' It is also clearly intended to recall the earlier statement (16.23) that the counsel which Ahithophel gave was 'as when one consults the word of God'. In 17.14 the author, who evidently holds 'good counsel' in the highest estimation, qualifies his admiration with the admission that God can and does overrule it. This corresponds exactly to the teaching of Proverbs, where side by side with

---

[13] On these passages see von Rad, 'Beginnings', pp. 198ff.

statements which accord the highest praise to human counsel, we find the following assertion:

> No wisdom, no understanding, no counsel
> Can avail against Yahweh. (21.30)

Yet the very fewness of these editorial comments testifies to a firm determination on the part of the author of the Succession Narrative to refrain from any suggestion that Yahweh achieves his purpose by constant interference with the natural course of events. It is his view that, within the general and all-embracing divine purpose, men are free to act as they please, and that their individual fates are determined by the natural working of retribution. In this view he is in complete agreement with the teaching of the proverbs quoted in the foregoing section on retribution.[14]

It might be argued against this attempt to show that the views of the Succession Narrative and Proverbs on retribution and providence are identical, that there is a wide difference between the two books in the way in which these beliefs are applied. The Succession Narrative is concerned wholly with their exemplification within the history of Israel; Proverbs never mentions Israel or its history, and appears to concern itself only with the careers and problems of individuals. But the difference is only apparent. The view that Proverbs, and the wisdom literature generally, are uninterested in Israel and its history rests upon a misunderstanding of their purpose. Proverbs can only be understood in relation to the situation for which it was compiled: the education of young men who were Israelites, and who were to be concerned in the political affairs of Israel. Its various collections were used as school textbooks; but obviously their teaching represents only a small part of the curriculum. It is evident that the syllabus included a number of other subjects, beginning with the elementary disciplines of reading and writing and going on to a range of subjects corresponding to those which we know to have been taught in the schools of the neighbouring states.[15] It

---

[14] Pp. 61f., *supra*.

[15] See p. 3, n. 12, *supra*. In addition, A. Klostermann's 'Schulwesen im alten Israel' (*Theologische Studien Th. Zahn ... dargebracht*, Leipzig, 1908, pp. 193-232) provides some interesting details concerning education in Israel; but, like Dürr (*op. cit.*) he was unaware of the extent to which Israelite scribal education was organized during the pre-exilic period, since it was then generally believed that the whole of the wisdom literature is post-exilic.

is probable that the history of Israel was included; for this, other textbooks may have been available.

It is for this reason that the scope of Proverbs is limited. It was compiled for use in connexion with that part of the curriculum which today would be called by such names as philosophy, psychology and sociology: it provided the pupils with precepts which helped them to understand human nature and gave them a guide to social and professional behaviour. Such teaching, illustrated though it is in Proverbs mainly with examples from the life of the individual, is also applicable to political life; and the book does, as we have seen, contain some specifically political instruction. The education of a Hushai and an Ahithophel—that is, of men who had the responsibility of guiding the political fortunes of Israel—will have included the study of such precepts as we have in Proverbs. The Succession Narrative, which demonstrates these precepts in action in the political and court life of Israel, thus shows itself to belong to the same milieu as the Book of Proverbs.

4. *Attitude towards the cult*

The emphasis placed by the authors of both Proverbs and the Succession Narrative on God's unseen control of human destiny through the natural course of events rather than through direct intervention inevitably affected their attitude towards the traditional means of communication between God and man provided by the cult. In the case of the Succession Narrative this was first noticed by Rost, whose conclusion was later confirmed by von Rad.[16] Rost made a detailed comparison of the place given to cultic activity in the Succession Narrative with that given to it in the other stories concerning David in the Books of Samuel. In the former, although semi-religious customs like fasting and weeping (II Sam. 12.16ff.) and mourning for the dead (13.31, 36; 14.2), the making of vows (15.7ff.) and the use of the altar as a place of sanctuary (I Kings 1.50ff.; 2.28ff.) are taken for granted, as also is the anointing of Solomon as king, it is significant that two aspects of cultic life which play a most important part in the other stories about David receive little attention: the Ark and the oracle.

[16] Rost, pp. 235, 239f.; von Rad, 'Beginnings', p. 202.

The Ark is referred to only twice: II Sam. 11.11; 15.24ff. The first reference occurs in a speech of Uriah the Hittite, and does no more than inform us that the Ark at this period was still carried into battle,[17] and that such a man as Uriah regarded it with great devotion. It helps the reader to form a picture of the character of Uriah, but it tells him nothing about the author's attitude towards the Ark or about the attitude of David as he is represented to us by the author.

The second reference (15.24-29) is more significant: here we are told of David's attitude towards the Ark, an attitude which is transparently that of the author also. The incident is capable of more than one explanation; but clearly David is—as also on an earlier occasion, II Sam. 12.20-23—acting here in an unexpected way and in accordance with new and unexpected theological beliefs. The priests who brought the Ark from Jerusalem to accompany David on his flight evidently believed that Yahweh's favour was in some way directly connected with the physical presence of the Ark—an idea which is certainly implied in the story of the bringing of the Ark to Jerusalem (II Sam. 6). But the author, expressing his own views through the words of David, appears to reject this belief: the Ark may be sent back to the city, where Absalom, now the master of Jerusalem, might well claim its presence as a sign that Yahweh's favour had now been transferred to him: but this is not so. Yahweh's favour is quite independent of possession of the cult-object; it is bestowed according to his inscrutable will:

'Carry the ark of God back into the city. If I find favour in the eyes of Yahweh, he will bring me back and let me see both it and his habitation; but if he says, "I have no pleasure in you", behold, here I am, let him do to me what seems good to him.'

Here we find a belief which tallies with the author's views on the mode of Yahweh's activity in history. The Ark is not, admittedly, cast aside as of no importance; but Yahweh's favour is independent of it, and will be shown, if it is to be shown, through events.

If it were not for this striking passage, the paucity of references to the Ark in the Succession Narrative might be explained by the difference in the subjects with which the two main collections

---

[17] Even this has been questioned, e.g. by McKane, *ad loc.*

of stories about David deal: the story of the bringing of the Ark to Jerusalem accounts for a large proportion of the references to it in the earlier parts of Samuel. This argument cannot, however, be used to explain the curious situation with regard to the consultation of the will of Yahweh through the oracle. In the other stories, David is recorded as having 'enquired of Yahweh' by this means on at least eight separate occasions.[18] These were all moments of crisis and decision. The Succession Narrative is not lacking in critical moments, yet not once—not even when he took the momentous decision to abandon Jerusalem to Absalom —are we told that David enquired of Yahweh. This practice is mentioned only once, obliquely, in a proverbial expression (II Sam. 16.23) as a well known custom. This difference cannot be explained as due to a change in the religious situation after David brought the Ark and installed it in Jerusalem, for if that were so we should expect to find that he consulted Yahweh in its presence, as—for example—it is recorded that Hezekiah did during the Assyrian crisis (II Kings 19.14ff.). There is no record of any such consultation in the Succession Narrative.

The only specific reference to a regular place of worship in the book is in II Sam. 15.32, which mentions a place on the summit of the Mount of Olives 'where one used to worship (*yištaḥᵃwe*) God'. This was probably a disused sanctuary, not necessarily dedicated to Yahweh: the word 'God', not 'Yahweh', is used here. The fact that it was while climbing the hill towards this sanctuary that David uttered a prayer (vv. 30f.) which was answered by the sudden arrival of Hushai just as he reached it may possibly be an indication that the author was not wholly indifferent to the special significance of holy places; but even here the means of communication with God was through a private prayer which was not made at the sanctuary itself, but some distance away from it; and there is no mention of an answer or assurance from God made through cultic means: the answer is provided through the perfectly natural, if providential, arrival of Hushai.

It may also be significant that there is no record in the book of David's offering sacrifice. The only sacrifices which are recorded are offered by the rebels, Absalom and Adonijah (II Sam. 15.12; I Kings 1.9). There is, however, one example of a divine

---

[18] I Sam. 22.10; 23.2, 4; 30.8; II Sam. 2.1; 5.19, 23; 21.1.

message to David which might be said to have been conveyed to him through cultic means. This is the oracle of Nathan in II Sam. 12, and it is the one great exception to the general rule. The author evidently respected the prophetic office as represented by Nathan.

In distinction from the paucity of references to formal cultic activity, there are in the book two examples of a direct appeal by David to God in prayer without any intermediary or special cultic apparatus: his fasting and humiliation on behalf of his son (II Sam. 12.16ff.) and his prayer that Yahweh would frustrate the counsel of Ahithophel (II Sam. 15.31). These might be taken to suggest that the author set more store by private prayer than by more formal cultic activity; and this would correspond well to his view of Yahweh's activity in history as unseen and continuous.

To sum up, we may say that the author of the Succession Narrative has a strong tendency, in conformity with his view of God's activity in human affairs, to push the cult into the background as a means of communication between God and man and to stress, through his portrayal of David, humility and a right personal relationship with God as the main, if not the only, needful thing.[19]

On the other hand, this tendency must not be overstated. Von Rad's assertion that for the author of the Succession Narrative 'the conception of Yahweh's activity through the ancient sacral institutions has become obsolete'[20] is undoubtedly such an overstatement. It is difficult to believe that such 'sacral persons' as Zadok and Nathan would have subscribed to this view, and the court at Jerusalem was hardly large enough to accommodate two entirely opposing views on the subject; nor is there any suggestion in the narrative that there was any such conflict of views. Moreover the king himself was a 'sacral person', whose status was enshrined in the theological statement of II Sam. 7, with which all at court may be said to have been familiar. It was presumably in accordance with this theological belief that Zadok and Nathan anointed Solomon at Gihon (I Kings 1.38-40). What we have in the Succession Narrative, therefore, is not a rejection of the sacral institutions but the appearance side by side with them of a new attitude towards God's activity in history which inevitably tended to diminish their importance.

[19] So Rost, pp. 239f.   [20] 'Beginnings', p. 204.

When we turn to Proverbs we find exactly the same situation. Here, too, the cult is not entirely ignored, but the references to it are very few. In the whole book there are three clear references to sacrifice. One of these (3.9f.)[21] states positively that sacrifice is necessary for the attainment of prosperity:

> Honour Yahweh with your wealth
> And with the first fruits of all your produce;
> Then your barns will be filled with grain,
> And your vats will be bursting with wine.

The other two are concerned only with the sacrifice (*zebaḥ*) of the wicked, which is classed among those actions which are 'abomination' (*tōʿēbā*) to Yahweh:

> The sacrifice of the wicked is an abomination to Yahweh,
> But the prayer of the upright is his delight. (15.8)

> The sacrifice of the wicked is an abomination;
> How much more when he brings it with evil intent! (21.27)

These passages must be taken to imply that sacrifice is considered to be a necessary practice, and beneficial when offered with a good intention; but it is significant that in 15.8 it is not the sacrifice of the upright which is contrasted with that of the wicked as giving delight to Yahweh, but his prayer.

The only other reference to cultic practices in Proverbs is 20.25, which refers to the making of vows (cf. II Sam. 15.7ff.), but again in a negative sense: it is a warning against doing this rashly.[22]

How is the extreme paucity of references to the cult in Proverbs to be accounted for? It might be argued that the cult lay outside the province of the wisdom teacher, and that therefore any *argumentum e silentio* is invalid. This would hold good if there were no references to the cult at all; but this is not so. The wisdom teachers evidently did consider it to be within their province to comment on the value of, and proper approach to, cultic activity, as one aspect of the 'way of life' which led to

---

[21] I regard this passage as roughly contemporary with Prov. 10-29. See my *Wisdom in Proverbs*, ch. 2, especially pp. 41-43.

[22] It may also be significant that the one occurrence of the word *kippēr* ('atone') in Proverbs refers to ethical and not cultic matters: 'By loyalty (*ḥesed*) and faithfulness (*ʾemet*) iniquity is atoned for' (16.6a). This was pointed out by R. B. Y. Scott, *op. cit.*, p. 24.

happiness and prosperity. Therefore the small amount of attention which they devote to this subject is significant. This is confirmed by the fact that in some of the non-Israelite wisdom literature the same phenomenon is observable. In the Egyptian *Instruction for King Merikare*[23] there are three, but only three references to the cult, and three also in the *Instruction of Ani*.[24] Thus in these works also, equally products of the scribal education, the cult has a place, *but a small one*, in the course of instruction. It is also of interest that, like the passages in Proverbs, these two works stress the greater importance of ethical conduct and prayer:

More acceptable (i.e. to God) is the virtue of one that is just of heart than the (sacrificial) ox of him that doeth iniquity. (*Merikare*; cf. Prov. 16.6a, quoted on p. 70, n. 22, *supra*.)

Pray with a loving heart, all the words whereof are hidden. Then he will hear what thou sayest and accept thine offering. (*Ani*; cf. Prov. 15.8, *supra*.)

5. Conclusion

There seem to be good grounds for concluding that on many fundamental matters—the importance attached to human wisdom and counsel both in public and private affairs; the acknowledgment of their limitations and of the unseen, all-embracing purpose of God and of his retributive justice; the relatively small attention paid to the cult; and the stress on the importance of ethical conduct, humility and private prayer—the Succession Narrative agrees closely with the scribal wisdom literature as represented by Proverbs rather than with the sacral tradition of Israel as reflected in—for example—the other Davidic stories in the Books of Samuel.

B. THE SUCCESSION NARRATIVE AS DIDACTIC LITERATURE

On the basis of this conclusion we may undertake a more detailed examination of the correspondences between Proverbs and the Succession Narrative. It is clear that they both reflect a common background in the court life of the early Israelite

[23] A. Erman, *The Literature of the Ancient Egyptians*, London, 1927, pp. 78, 79, 83; *ANET*, pp. 416, 417.

[24] Erman, *op. cit.*, pp. 235, 236, 239; *ANET*, p. 420.

monarchy. But it is possible that there may be an even closer connexion between them. The life of the court which the Succession Narrative depicts certainly reflects much of the teaching of Proverbs; but there is a further possibility, which may throw light on the hitherto unexplained literary skill of the author of the former, and the care which he bestowed—over and above the requirements of his political purpose—on characterization and psychological study. This is that it was his intention, through his characters and situations, not merely to reflect but to teach the doctrines of the wisdom schools. In other words, the question which will now be discussed is whether the author is to be regarded as himself a teacher, who has consciously created his characters and situations as concrete examples, in narrative form, of the teaching which we find in Proverbs.

1. The use of narrative in wisdom literature

There would be nothing new or incongruous about such a literary device. The dramatization of gnomic teaching in the form of stories in order to strike the imagination or the conscience of the listener or reader has always been a recognized educational method. A vivid account of the life of specific persons, embellished with circumstantial detail, is a hundred times more effective as a means of persuasion than a brief, bare statement of fact or principle, whether the purpose is to sell a commercial product or to teach a moral or religious lesson. The parable and the fable, two ubiquitous forms of this kind of teaching, are known to have been in use since at least the third millennium BC,[25] and in the Parable of Jotham in Judges 9.7-20 we have an early Israelite example.

Even in the simplest form of Old Testament wisdom literature —the single proverb—we have examples which show that the early wisdom teachers of Israel were aware of the effectiveness of vivid detail as a means of education.

The proverb, both in Israelite and foreign wisdom literature, normally assumed two distinct forms. In the exhortation or

---

[25] See J. J. A. van Dijk, La sagesse suméro-accadienne, Leiden, 1953; W. G. Lambert, Babylonian Wisdom Literature, Oxford, 1960. The oldest extant MSS of Sumerian fables, e.g. of the Fable of the Tamarisk and the Palm, mainly date from the Old Babylonian Period (c. 1700-1600 BC); but the literary genre itself is undoubtedly considerably older.

warning (*Mahnwort*) the pupil was warned to pursue or avoid a particular kind of conduct, e.g.

> Love not sleep, lest you come to poverty;
> Open your eyes, and you will have plenty of bread.
>
> (Prov. 20.13)

The 'statement' (*Aussagewort*) simply describes an action or situation, but makes no explicit appeal to the pupil, e.g.

> The sluggard does not plough in the autumn;
> He will seek at harvest and have nothing. (20.4)[26]

It is chiefly among the latter that we find attempts to dramatize the situation and so to appeal to the pupil's imagination by creating a vivid and lifelike scene, e.g.

> The sluggard dips his hand into the dish,
> And will not even bring it back to his mouth.
>
> (19.24; cf. 26.15)

> 'It is bad, it is bad', says the buyer;
> But when he goes away, then he boasts. (20.14)

> The sluggard says, 'There is a lion outside!
> I shall be slain in the streets!' (22.13; cf. 26.13)

In a few cases this treatment of a subject is extended to form a paragraph beyond the bounds of the simple proverb, as in the vivid description of over-indulgence in drink (Prov. 23.29-35) or the banquet sequence (23.1-8) which depicts a dinner party and (this time in the form of an exhortation) draws a moral about the proper behaviour of the guest. The longest of these scenes in the older wisdom literature of Israel is the description of the good wife in Prov. 31.10-31, which extends over 22 verses. Other examples are found in the older sections of Prov. 1-9: the four warnings against the 'strange woman' (2.16-19; 5.3-8; 6.24f., 32; 7.5, 25-27)[27] and the two contrasting pictures of the banquets offered to the young man by Wisdom (9.1-6) and the 'foolish woman' (9.13-18).

In course of time this desire for vivid portrayal of moral

---

[26] On these two types of proverb see W. Zimmerli, 'Zur Struktur der alttestamentlichen Weisheit', *ZAW* 51, 1933, p. 184.

[27] See Whybray, *op. cit.* and 'Some Literary Problems in Proverbs I-IX', *VT* 16, 1966, pp. 482-496.

lessons led to a variety of experiments. The authors of the later parts of Prov. 1-9 chose to present their teaching by means of a personification of wisdom in the guise of a woman[28] who stands in the street and offers lifegiving instruction to young men in competition with the other women of the street whose invitations lead to ruin and death (1.20-33; 8). Another device was that of autobiography: the wisdom teacher describes to his pupils either his past exemplary life or some incidents which he has observed from which moral lessons can be drawn. The autobiographical form had its origins in Egypt, where kings—e.g. in the *Instruction for Merikare* and the *Instruction of Amenemhet*—or ordinary individuals, in their tomb inscriptions,[29] are represented as describing their experiences or their exemplary lives.[30] Proverbs 1-9 contains one such example of a wisdom teacher's testimony to his pupils about his own exemplary education:

> For I also was a weak child,
> An only one, in my father's care;
> And he taught me and said unto me,
> 'Let thy heart hold fast my words;
> Keep my commandments, forget them not,
> And turn not away from the words of my mouth.'
>
> (Prov. 4.3-5)[31]

The more extended autobiographical lesson does not occur in the early period of Israelite wisdom literature; but at a later date the so-called 'memoirs' of Nehemiah seem to owe something to this tradition,[32] and it appears later still in Ecclesiastes, especially 1.12-2.17, and in the Wisdom of Solomon, chs. 7-9.

[28] For the origins of this figure see Whybray, *op. cit.*, ch. 4.

[29] See the examples in Brunner, *Erziehung*, pp. 153ff.

[30] In Israel it is possible that this type of moral teaching was also influenced by the cultic thanksgivings (e.g. Ps. 18; 34; 40.9f., etc.) in which the worshipper, who has been delivered from his trouble, tells the congregation of his experiences.

[31] For this reconstruction of a defective text see Whybray, *op. cit.*, pp. 44f. This passage seems to have been modelled on Egyptian prototypes, e.g. 'My father also trained me in the useful writings which had come down to him. Then I found that men praised me, since I had become wise, since my eyes had been opened' (an Egyptian Middle Kingdom text, quoted in Brunner, *Erziehung*, pp. 158f.).

[32] The double motive of self-justification and the setting of an example of conduct to others in the Nehemiah Memoirs is identical with that of the Egyptian instructions and tomb-inscriptions mentioned above, although there is no reason to suspect direct Egyptian influence in this case.

The device of the wisdom teacher's account of his own observation of others rather than of his own exemplary life does, however, occur fairly early. It appears to have developed its own characteristic style and vocabulary, especially the 'I saw' (*rā'ītī*; *wā'ēre'*) formula; and the use of the word '*ābar*, 'pass by':

> I passed by (*ā'bartī*) the field of the sluggard,
> By the vineyard of the man without sense (*ḥᵃsar-lēb*);
> And lo, it was all overgrown with thorns;
> The ground was covered with nettles,
> And its stone wall was broken down.
> Then I saw and considered it;
> I looked (*rā'ītī*) and received instruction (*mūsār*).
>
> (Prov. 24.30-32)

Then follows the moral (vv. 35f.).

Another example, from a wisdom psalm:

> I have seen (*rā'ītī*) a wicked man overbearing,
> And towering like a cedar of Lebanon.
> Again I passed by (*wā'e'ᵉbōr*)[33] and lo, he was no more;
> Though I sought him, he could not be found. (Ps. 37.35f.)

The most elaborate example in Proverbs is 7.6-23,[34] which begins with the words

> At the window of my house
> I have looked out through my lattice,
> And I have seen (*wā'ēre'*) among the simple,
> I have perceived among the youths
> A young man without sense (*ḥᵃsar-lēb*)

and tells a complete story, with much circumstantial detail, of the seduction of a young man by an unprincipled woman, ending with the moral that those who yield to such enticements meet an untimely death.

Finally the two forms—the autobiographical revelation and the example given by the teacher of his own observation of others—were combined in Ecclesiastes, where in 1.12-2.17 the wisdom teacher, in the guise of Solomon, offers to his pupils an account both of his own spiritual pilgrimage and of his observation of others: 'I have seen (*rā'ītī*) everything that is done under the sun;

---

[33] Following Versions.
[34] See Whybray, *art. cit.*, pp. 482-486.

and behold, all is vanity' (1.14); 'And whatever my eyes desired I did not keep from them; I kept my heart from no pleasure' (2.10). The same combination is found in the Wisdom of Solomon (chs. 7-9).

The principle which underlies the autobiographical form is a very ancient one: the wisdom teacher is an old man, who has seen much of life and had ample opportunity to reflect on what he has seen. Now in his old age he hands on the fruit of his experiences to the young. When the autobiographical claim is made in the name of some famous figure from the past, such as a king (Amenemhet, Solomon) or a great statesman (Ptahhotep, Ahiqar)[35] a further refinement is added: through both the prestige and the historical concreteness of the supposed author the teaching given is more likely to be readily assimilated by the pupil.

The vividness, and therefore the effectiveness, of such instruction could, however, be increased even more if it was presented in the form of a narrative about such famous people: in other words, in a story about the past which claimed to be a historical account of their lives. Experiments with this genre were made in Egypt long before the birth of Israelite wisdom literature: in the *Instruction of Amenemhet* the old king, the first Pharaoh of the Twelfth Dynasty,[36] is represented as offering to his son and successor an account of the historical events of his reign, mingled with advice; and in the *Instruction for Merikare* another king, probably of the 22nd century BC, does the same thing.[37] In these two works, however, the blending of narrative with moral teaching is incomplete: morals are drawn from the events described, but the narrative itself is hardly used as the vehicle of the instruction.

2. *The Joseph Narrative and the Succession Narrative*

It seems to have been left to the Israelites to perfect this genre. Von Rad has shown[38] that the Joseph Narrative (Gen. 37; 39-50) in its present form is quite different from the other patriarchal

---

[35] *The Instruction of Ptahhotep*, Erman, *op. cit.*, pp. 54-66; *ANET*, pp. 412-414; *The Words of Ahiqar*, in A. E. Cowley, *Aramaic Papyri of the Fifth Century BC*, Oxford, 1923, pp. 204-248; *ANET*, pp. 427-430.
[36] Died c. 1960 BC. The earliest MSS are from 1500-1200 (J. A. Wilson in *ANET*, p. 418). See further, pp. 108f., 110ff., *infra*.
[37] MS from the 15th century BC (Wilson in *ANET*, p. 414).
[38] 'Joseph Narrative and Ancient Wisdom', pp. 292-300.

stories. It is 'a novel through and through'[39]; a 'didactic wisdom story'[40] in which the hero, Joseph, is represented as a perfect example of the application of the scribal ideal which was the goal of the educational programme of the wisdom schools. Von Rad compared the character and career of Joseph with the teaching of the wisdom literature, both Egyptian and Israelite, but especially with Proverbs, and pointed out how closely the two correspond. Joseph's skill in speech, ability to give good counsel to kings, knowledge when to speak and when to conceal his thoughts, modesty, humility, self-discipline, patience, resistance to the unlawful advances of women and godly fear—all these characteristics belong to the scribal ideal taught in Proverbs; and as a consequence of all these virtues Joseph attains that complete pre-eminence in his profession, and that unadulterated happiness which the wisdom teachers promise to those pupils who accept and follow their teaching. The Joseph Narrative also resembles wisdom literature in its broad human interest, in its realism and concern with what is practicable in human affairs, and in its emancipation from the fetters of a narrow attachment to a spirituality centred on the cult and on the old sacral traditions.

Von Rad also found a close relationship between the 'underlying theological presuppositions'[41] of the Joseph Narrative and early wisdom literature. Both are 'notoriously sparing of theological pronouncements', of which the former contains only two, put into the mouth of Joseph: Gen. 45.5ff. and 50.20. These express a belief in an all-embracing divine guidance of human destiny whose operation is not only beyond man's control but also beyond his understanding—a belief which seems to be curiously in conflict with the view implied in the rest of the narrative, that a man's destiny lies in his own hands in the sense that he can infallibly achieve eventual happiness and prosperity by following certain known rules of conduct which operate on a purely natural plane. The author thus reveals a contradiction existing in his own mind. This, however, is not a contradiction peculiar to this writer: the same contradiction is found, according to von Rad, in the wisdom literature; and he cites examples from both Egyptian wisdom instructions and Proverbs of a doctrine of the purpose of God which overrules the plans of men. His examples from Proverbs are the same as those which we have cited in our dis-

[39] P. 292.   [40] P. 300.   [41] Pp. 296ff.

cussion of this aspect of the Succession Narrative (16.9; 19.21;
20.24; 21.30).[42]

Von Rad's thesis about the Joseph Narrative is of significance
for the study of the Succession Narrative. If his view is correct,
that we have here in the Old Testament an example of an extended
narrative about a historical character from Israel's past which is
not in any sense a piece of historical writing but a 'novel' composed for the wisdom schools in order to give force to their
teaching through a portrayal of the exemplary character of its
hero, the similarity which we have discovered between the ideas
of the Succession Narrative and that same wisdom teaching
suggests the possibility that the Succession Narrative also may
have been written with—among others—a similar purpose in
mind.

3. *The Succession Narrative as a dramatization of proverbial wisdom*

The difference in the subject chosen meant that any proverbial
material which the author of the Succession Narrative might use
would have to be handled quite differently from the way in
which it was handled in the Joseph Narrative. The author of the
latter chose as his hero a semi-legendary figure from the remote
past, concerning whom the existing traditions were probably
scanty[43] and still sufficiently flexible to allow for expansion and

[42] Von Rad, however, makes a sharp distinction between the theological
standpoints of the Joseph Narrative and the Succession Narrative. In the
latter's theological statements about the all-embracing purpose of God
('Beginnings', pp. 198ff.; cf. my discussion on pp. 60-66, *supra*) he sees
no more than a 'theological tension' in the author's mind—a tension which
'no one can help feeling who has any real faith' (p. 202): in spite of the belief
there expressed in God's hidden purpose, 'men do not sink to the status of
puppets'. Yet in the Joseph Narrative he feels that there is more than a
theological tension: 'a deep cleavage threatens to arise between the divine
and human purposes, and . . . human activity is so heavily fettered by the
all-embracing control of events that it comes perilously near to losing all
significance whatever' (p. 298). It would appear that the basis of the distinction between the two works in von Rad's view is that the Joseph Narrative, unlike the Succession Narrative, is 'devoid of any specifically theological interest in redemptive history' (p. 299). But it is doubtful whether
this view can be maintained, since the author of the Joseph Narrative deliberately chose for his hero a figure whose place in redemptive history was
already fixed and known to his readers. It does not seem to me that the
theological tension in the Joseph Narrative is greater than that which we
find in the Succession Narrative.

[43] On the origins of the Joseph theme see M. Noth, *Überlieferungsgeschichte
des Pentateuch*, Stuttgart, 1948, pp. 226-232.

embellishment. He was therefore able to exercise his imagination very freely and so to write a story which was nearer to pure fiction than to the genre of the historical novel. The writer of the Succession Narrative, on the other hand, was limited in his choice of subject by his primary aim, which was to write a political work dealing with a period which was still within living memory. He could neither write pure fiction nor concentrate on a single hero whom he was free to represent as a paragon. Even though one man was to be the central character, his story must be about a whole generation of men and women whose characters were to some extent known to his readers; it must deal, broadly speaking, with known historical events, and it must faithfully portray the customs, behaviour and atmosphere of the Israel, and especially the Israelite court, of the author's own time. Moreover, any didactic purpose which he might have must not be allowed to obscure his main purpose, which was to support the dynasty of David and its contemporary representative, Solomon.

But these limiting circumstances also provided some advantages, which the author used to the full. The method used in the Joseph Narrative, of concentrating on a single man and making him an example of all the virtues taught by the wisdom schools had disadvantages as an educational method. Joseph is too good to be true: he is hardly recognizable as a real human being. Moreover, although he embodies every virtue, the fact that the other characters pale into insignificance beside him means that the situations in which he is placed have no reality: everything is in black and white, and there is none of the stuff of human conflict and challenge which constituted the real world in which the pupils in the schools would be required to put their theoretical knowledge into practice. For this reason the Joseph Narrative is a very colourless affair compared with the actual proverbial teaching which it is intended to exemplify. The Book of Proverbs is, as Duesberg remarked,[44] in itself a *comédie humaine*: a host of characters appear in its pages, and these are the characters and situations of the real world. It is true that they also are usually painted in black and white: such is the nature of the proverb, which distils and abstracts real life into a tiny compass. Nevertheless they are extremely varied: not merely do we have the obvious contrasts between the fool and the wise, the righteous

[44] *Op. cit.*, p. 265.

and the wicked, but we find the street gang of youths, the loitering prostitute and the weak young man, the thief, the adulterer, the husband absent on business, the farmer, the sluggard, the dishonest trader, the strict father, the poor and the rich, the counsellor, the debtor and the creditor, the royal messenger and many more characters taken from life.

The characters in the Succession Narrative do not correspond entirely to those of Proverbs: they almost all belong to a particular class in society, and are shown mainly not in the circumstances of their private lives but at court and about the business of politics; nevertheless they are all recognizably real characters shown in real situations. More important still, they are—with the exception of some of the minor ones—shown as a mixture of wisdom and folly, of goodness and wickedness. The necessity of depicting real people in his book provided the author with an opportunity to show how the precepts of the wisdom schools were to be worked out in real situations in the very court in which the pupils would spend their lives; and to depict, not merely a solitary model of virtue but a great variety of examples both of wisdom which they could emulate, and of folly from which they could take warning.

At the same time, the other side of the wisdom teaching which is reflected in the book, concerning God's hidden guidance of human destiny, fitted extremely well with the author's purpose. In the Joseph Narrative this is expressed in rather general terms:

'God sent me before you to preserve for you a remnant on earth. . . . So it was not you who sent me here, but God.' (Gen. 45.7f.)

'You meant evil against me; but God meant it for good, to bring it about that many people should be kept alive.' (50.20)

In the Succession Narrative this becomes a concrete and specific purpose directed towards the establishment and maintenance of the Davidic dynasty. God overrules in a mysterious way, and without interfering with natural causation, both the wickedness and folly of David and the plans of the dynastic rivals who seek for themselves the throne which God has already determined to give to Solomon.

The writing of a historical novel on the scale and with the range of the Succession Narrative presented the author with a task for which there were no real precedents in Israelite writing.

To a large extent it must be a work of the imagination: the author must draw on his experience of people and situations, and adapt this to fit the imaginary scenes which he was creating. But the way in which he looked at life was conditioned by the education which he had received. He had been trained to seek guidance in every situation from the stock of proverbs which he had been taught; consequently when he created imaginary scenes, his mind was filled with this proverbial teaching, and he tended to use those proverbs as a starting-point and bring them to life.[45]

The proverbial influence can be seen both in form and content. With regard to form, several of the types most frequently found in Proverbs are represented in the Succession Narrative.

The *simile*. Proverbs contains many examples of this, e.g.:

> Like a gold ring in a swine's snout
> Is a beautiful woman without discretion. (11.22)

> Pleasant words are like a honeycomb,
> Sweetness to the soul and health to the body. (16.24)

> The purpose in a man's mind is like deep water,
> But a man of understanding will draw it out. (20.5)

The Succession Narrative contains one example of a simile in strict proverbial form which is undoubtedly a genuine proverb, although it does not occur in any extant collection[46]:

> We are like water spilt on the ground,
> Which cannot be gathered up again. (II Sam. 14.14)

Other similes are rather reflections of proverbs than actual proverbs:

My lord the king is like the angel of God to discern good and evil. (II Sam. 14.17)

My lord has wisdom like the wisdom of the angel of God to know all things that are on the earth. (14.20)

The counsel which Ahithophel gave was as when one consults the word of God. (16.23)

There is, as one might expect, a particularly large concentration of similes in the speeches of the two professional counsellors, Ahithophel and Hushai, which in other respects also betray the

[45] Cf. McKenzie, *art. cit.*, p. 3.
[46] On this see Cazelles, *art. cit.*, pp. 33f.

author's intimate acquaintance with and mastery of the wisdom of the schools:

I will bring all the people back to you as a bride comes home to her husband. (17.3a)

Even the valiant man, whose heart is like the heart of a lion, will utterly melt with fear. (17.10)

We shall light upon him as the dew falls on the ground. (17.12)

One of these employs, though in a different context, imagery which occurs in Proverbs:

They are enraged, like a bear robbed of her cubs. (II Sam. 17.8)

Compare:

> Let a man meet a bear robbed of her cubs
> Rather than a fool in his folly. (Prov. 17.12)

The comparison. Proverbs frequently compares two objects or situations in order to enable the reader to discern relative values. This is usually expressed by the formula *ṭōb* ... *min* ... ('Better is ... than ...'), e.g.

> Better is a little with the fear of Yahweh
> Than great treasure and trouble with it. (Prov. 15.16)

> Better is a dinner of herbs where love is
> Than a fatted ox and hatred with it. (15.17)

> Better is a neighbour who is near
> Than a brother who is far away. (27.10b)

The same kind of comparison and contrast, also between love and hatred and presence and absence, is found in two passages in the Succession Narrative:

The hatred with which he hated her was greater than the love with which he had loved her. (II Sam. 13.15)

Absalom concludes that exile is preferable to presence in Jerusalem without the king's love:

Why have I come from Geshur? It would be better for me to be there still. (14.32)

We also find in Proverbs another phenomenon which is significantly exemplified in the Succession Narrative: pairs of

proverbs which appear to contradict one another absolutely.
These pairs are usually found in different parts of the book; but
occasionally they are placed side by side; and this suggests that
the contradiction is deliberate[47]:

> Answer not a fool according to his folly,
> Lest you be like him yourself.
> Answer a fool according to his folly,
> Lest he be wise in his own eyes. (Prov. 26.4f.)

This phenomenon probably points to a particular aspect of the
education of the counsellor: he was expected to be able, as the
occasion demanded, to argue on either side of a debate. In the
speeches of Ahithophel and Hushai the author of the Succession
Narrative has clearly demonstrated his ability to do this; and
these two speeches appear to be expansions of two such mutually
contradictory proverbs: Ahithophel argues that swift action gains
the victory, and Hushai that a prudent man does not rush into
action!

Apart from ch. 17, which is obviously itself to be classed as
wisdom literature, some of the examples given above might be
dismissed as nothing more than common conversational forms
having no direct relationship to the scribal education, were it not
for two considerations: the vivid imagery closely resembles that
of the proverb, and the themes—death, knowledge, wisdom, love
and hatred, father and son—also belong to the same world of
thought. Both in form and in content, proverbial influence can
be seen.

In some passages, even where the proverbial form is entirely
lacking, the situation described strikes the reader forcibly as
proverbial in character: the bizarre image in II Sam. 17.13 of 'all
Israel' dragging a city stone by stone into the valley is most
easily explained if we suppose it to be based on a proverb which
taught that while small numbers can achieve little, a multitude
working with a common purpose is irresistible; and we may see
other proverbial situations in the love which turns to hatred in
II Sam. 13.15; in David's idleness which breeds lust in II Sam.
11.2; in the contrast between a true friend and a treacherous son
in 15.19-22; in the folly of mourning on a day of victory in
19.2ff.; and in many other scenes.

[47] On this phenomenon and its significance see von Rad, *Theology* I, pp. 422f.

The examples discussed above suggest in a general way that the author's education in the wisdom school influenced his writing and contributed to his literary inspiration. But we can go further. In many cases it is possible to show that proverbs extant in the Book of Proverbs have been dramatized in the Succession Narrative.

These correspondences can be discerned in three major areas:

1. Wisdom and folly.
2. The education of children.
3. The king.

In addition, the two books have many subsidiary themes in common[48]: friendship and enmity, idleness, rich and poor, humility, death, evil companions, quarrels, man's insecurity, messengers, old age, pride, treachery and loyalty are among them. We shall consider the correspondences first under the three main headings, and then give some examples from the minor themes.

1. *Wisdom and folly*

(*a*) *Patience and the control of the temper.*

> The vexation of a fool is known at once,
> But the prudent man ignores an insult. (Prov. 12.16)

> He who is slow to anger is better than the mighty,
> And he who rules his spirit than he who takes a city. (16.32)

(Cf. also 13.16; 14.17 LXX; 17.27.)

So Absalom, learning of the rape of Tamar and determined to avenge this crime, 'spoke to Amnon neither good nor bad', and waited patiently for two years for a suitable occasion (II Sam. 13.22).

(*b*) *Prudent consideration before taking action.*

> The simple man believes everything,
> But the prudent man looks where he is going. (Prov. 14.15)

> A prudent man sees danger and hides himself,
> But the simple go on and pay for it. (27.12)

Such a 'simple man' was Adonijah, who rushed to his destruction

[48] I.e., subsidiary in one or both of the books.

through his unconsidered request for the hand of Abishag (I Kings 2.13ff.). David's adultery and Amnon's rape were also unconsidered acts of folly.

(*c*) *The ability to learn from experience.*

> Like a dog that returns to its own vomit
> Is a fool who repeats his folly. (Prov. 26.11)

> Though you crush a fool in a mortar,
> Yet his folly will never depart from him. (27.22)

Again Adonijah, who was unable to learn the lesson of his earlier narrow escape, but foolishly incurred Solomon's wrath a second time (I Kings 2.13ff.) provides an exact illustration.

(*d*) *The avoidance of treacherous companions.*

> He who walks with wise men ($h^a k\bar{a}m\bar{\imath}m$) becomes wise,
> But the companion of fools will suffer harm. (Prov. 13.20)

> A man of violence entices his friend ($r\bar{e}a'$)
> And leads him into a way that is not good. (16.29)

(Cf. also Prov. 1.10, 'My son, if sinners entice you, do not consent'.)

Amnon's readiness to listen to the advice of his 'friend' ($r\bar{e}a'$, II Sam. 13.3) and its consequences provide a perfect example of this. The statement that Jonadab is 'very wise' ($h\bar{a}k\bar{a}m$ $m^{e'}\bar{o}d$) is probably ironical: wisdom is not mere ingenuity; cleverness, unless it counts the consequences, is really folly.

(*e*) *Humility versus pride and ambition.*

> When pride comes, then comes disgrace;
> But with the humble there is wisdom. (Prov. 11.2)

> Pride goes before destruction,
> And a haughty spirit before a fall. (16.18)

(Cf. also 16.5; 29.23.)

The pride and ambition of Absalom, and of Adonijah who 'exalted himself' (I Kings 1.5), is clearly an exemplification of these proverbs.

(*f*) *Control of sexual passion.* The warnings against adultery in Proverbs occur mainly in chs. 1-9 (5.3-23; 6.24-35; 7.5-27), but

mainly belong to the older wisdom. They are too lengthy to
quote in full. Their twin themes are the folly of the adulterer and
the certainty that his action will lead to disgrace and even death.
David's and Amnon's unlawful passions clearly come under these
condemnations. Outside chs. 1-9 the strictures of Proverbs on
this subject are concerned mainly with self-control, the character
of the loose woman, and the special case of the libidinous king:

> A man without self-control
> Is like a city broken into and left without walls. (Prov. 25.28)

> A harlot is a deep pit;
> The wife of another man is a narrow well. (23.27)

> Give not your strength to women,
> Your loins to those who destroy kings. (31.3)

We may also see in II Sam. 11.4, which records laconically and
without comment how Bathsheba returned to her house after her
adultery, an intentional reflexion on the amorality of women such
as she who is portrayed in Prov. 30.20:

> This is the way of an adulteress:
> She eats, and wipes her mouth,
> And says, 'I have done no wrong'.

(*g*) *The use of speech.* A man's words, according to both the wisdom
literature and the Succession Narrative, are the expression of his
character and the chief cause of his success or downfall. Wise
speech in the form of counsel given to kings has already been
considered[49]; but there are many specific scenes in the Succession
Narrative which correspond to particular proverbs.

The *speech of the wise woman of Tekoa* (II Sam. 14.4ff.), behind
which lies the wisdom of Joab, is an excellent example of the way
to use words to persuade a king:

> With patience a ruler may be persuaded,
> And a soft tongue will break a bone. (Prov. 25.15)

Absalom's promises to the litigants about what he would do if he
were judge in the land (II Sam. 15.4) are, besides being an
example of persuasive speech, also an example of empty promises
of which one should beware:

[49] Pp. 57ff., *supra.*

Like clouds and wind without rain
Is a man who boasts of a gift he does not give. (Prov. 25.14)

Ziba's seizing the most favourable moment to further his interests by telling lies about Meribbaal (II Sam. 16.1-4) is an example of the 'word in season':

To make an apt answer is a joy to a man,
And a word in season, how good it is! (Prov. 15.23)

A word fitly spoken
Is like apples of gold in a setting of silver. (25.11)

If, on the other hand—and the author leaves us in doubt on this point—Ziba is telling the truth, then his action in bringing assistance to David is an example of the behaviour of the wise servant:

An intelligent servant will rule over a son who behaves shamefully,
And will share the inheritance (cf. II Sam. 19.29) as one of the brothers.
(Prov. 17.2)

Not only does *Hushai's speech* (II Sam. 17.7-13) illustrate the fact that

Pleasant speech increases persuasiveness. (Prov. 16.21b),

but, coming after Ahithophel's speech, which at first 'pleased Absalom and all the elders of Israel' (v. 4), it illustrates in a humorous way the adage that

He who states his case first seems right,
Until another comes and questions him. (Prov. 18.17)

Joab's fateful rebuke of David (II Sam. 19.5-7) illustrates the dilemma which faced the conscientious courtier: if he gave frank but unpalatable advice, would he be praised for his wisdom, or punished for his audacity? It would seem that the wisdom teachers were well aware of this problem, and, as on some other occasions, they were unable to provide a solution, but contented themselves with setting down two mutually contradictory answers side by side. The whole scene in II Sam. 19.1-8 with its eventual consequences for Joab may be said to have been created as an illustration of this dilemma, which we find expressed in two *consecutive* proverbs, Prov. 14.35; 15.1:

SN G

An intelligent servant wins the king's favour,
But his wrath falls on one who behaves shamefully;

but on the other hand:

A soft answer turns away wrath,
But a harsh word stirs up anger.

Prov. 28.23 deals with the same question, and takes the optimistic view, in contrast to II Sam. 19:

A man who reproves others will afterwards acquire more favour
Than one who flatters with his tongue.

We may also note in Joab's speech another proverbial lesson: his warning that

'I swear by Yahweh, that if you do not go, not a man will stay with you this night; and this will be worse for you than all the evil which has come upon you from your youth until now'

exactly agrees with the statement in Prov. 14.28 that

A king's glory depends on the numbers of his people,
And without his people a prince is ruined.

2. *The education of children*

As has been remarked above,[50] the key to one of the major themes of the Succession Narrative—David's failure to control his children—is provided by the one specific reference in I Kings 1.6, where it is said of Adonijah that 'his father had never at any time displeased him by asking, "Why have you done this or that?" '. The failure to exercise proper discipline over children was one of the most signal examples of folly in the eyes of the wisdom teacher, and Proverbs abounds in references to this. In discipline (*mūsār*), which meant the unrelenting effort by parent and teacher to form the character of the young by both precept and the rod, lay the indispensable key to wisdom; and if it was unsuccessful and the pupil grew up heedless of what he had been taught, this was a tragedy both for him and for his parents. The author of the Succession Narrative makes it clear by implication that this was one of the main causes of the disgrace and death of Amnon, Absalom and Adonijah and of the broken heart of their

[50] P. 38, *supra.*

father. A few examples out of many from Proverbs will illustrate the identity on this matter of the points of view of the two books:

> He who spares the rod hates his son,
> But he who loves him is diligent to discipline him. (Prov. 13.24)

> Discipline your son while there is hope;
> Do not set your heart on his destruction. (19.18)

> Train up a child in the way he should go,
> And when he is old he will not depart from it. (22.6)

> Do not withhold discipline from a child;
> If you beat him with the rod, he will not die.
> If you beat him with the rod
> You will save his life from Sheol. (23.13f.)

(Cf. also 13.1; 15.5; 22.15; 29.15, etc.)

The tragic consequences of failure to exercise discipline which are depicted in the Succession Narrative are equally clearly portrayed in Proverbs:

> A stupid son is a grief to a father,
> And the father of a fool has no joy. (17.21)

> A foolish son is a grief to his father
> And bitterness to her who bore him. (17.25)

> He who does violence to his father and chases away his mother
> Is a son who causes shame and brings reproach. (19.26)

(Cf. also 15.20; 20.20; 23.24; 30.17, etc.)

3. *The ideal king*

The proper character of kingship was a matter of primary concern to the wisdom teachers, and also to the author of the Succession Narrative. There are two sections in Proverbs exclusively devoted to this subject: 25.1-7 and 31.1-9 (the 'words of Lemuel, king of Massa, which his mother taught him'), and many other proverbs in other parts of the book; and the Succession Narrative gives us, in the character of David, the fullest portrait of a king in the Old Testament.

Both books deal with a number of aspects of kingship. Some proverbs in the Book of Proverbs are evidently intended for the instruction of the king himself, or of the heir to the throne, and are of two kinds: those which give practical advice about the art of successful kingship, and those which remind the king of his responsibilities and of his relationship with God. Other proverbs are addressed rather to the courtiers, and are also of two kinds: those which give practical advice about the art of the courtier, and those which warn the courtier of the power of the king, especially of his power to destroy him. All these subjects receive full treatment in the Succession Narrative, and the general similarity of the two books in this respect is too obvious to need detailed exposition. But once more there are examples of a closer and more specific relationship.

(*a*) *The king's 'wisdom'*. On his deathbed David instructed Solomon to show his 'wisdom' by putting to death Joab and Shimei as men who were a danger or an embarrassment to the throne. Solomon did more: he also banished Abiathar; he put to death Adonijah, but only after letting him put himself in the wrong; and with Shimei also he found a specious pretext for his execution (I Kings 2.39-46). In this way Solomon demonstrated that his wisdom was, if anything, even greater than that of his father. In this he exemplifies the 'royal wisdom' recommended in Prov. 20.26:

> A wise (*ḥākām*) king winnows the wicked,
> And drives the wheel over them.

These chapters also vividly illustrate another phrase which we find in Proverbs, the 'messenger of death':

> The king's wrath is a messenger of death,
> And a wise man will appease it. (Prov. 16.14)

No clearer example of a 'messenger of death' could be found than Solomon's faithful servant Benaiah, who was employed to kill Adonijah, Joab and Shimei. The author conveys the ruthlessness of the royal power in each case with the laconic phrase, 'And he struck him down, and he died' (I Kings 2.25, 34, 46).[51] Joab, Shimei and Adonijah illustrate the second half of the proverb: they suffered for their folly in not appeasing the king's wrath. The reason for their execution, and perhaps the character of their executioner, is well illustrated by another proverb:

> An evil man seeks only rebellion,
> But a cruel messenger will be sent against him. (Prov. 17.11)

[51] There is a slight variation in v. 34: 'and killed him' for 'and he died'.

(*b*) *The king's responsibilities and relation to God.* The restriction by the overruling purpose of God of man's freedom to control events applies also to the king; and the way in which David at the end of his life, after years of inability to make up his mind about a successor, finds that events have conspired to force him to a decision, which is in fact that which Yahweh has already made, corresponds to the statement of Prov. 21.1 that

> The king's heart is a flowing stream in the hand of Yahweh;
> He turns it wherever he will.

The conception of the king's duty to administer justice to rich and poor alike which is the theme of Nathan's parable and David's reply (II Sam. 12.1-6) and also of David's reply to the request of the woman of Tekoa (14.8-11) is the same as that of Proverbs:

> Like a roaring lion or a charging bear
> Is a wicked ruler over a poor people. (28.15)

> If a king judges the poor with equity
> His throne will be established for ever. (29.14)

> Open your mouth on behalf of the dumb,
> For the rights of all who are left without protection.
> Open your mouth, judge righteously,
> Maintain the rights of the poor and needy. (31.8f.)

The confidence of the woman of Tekoa that the king is endowed with special wisdom in making judgments (II Sam. 14.17, 20) seems also to be the meaning of Prov. 16.10:

> Inspired decisions (*qesem*) are on the lips of the king;
> His mouth does not err when he sits in judgment.[52]

The view of the author of the Succession Narrative that Absalom's rebellion was a punishment for David's sin is echoed in Proverbs:

> When a man's ways please Yahweh,
> He makes even his enemies to be at peace with him. (16.7)

> It is an abomination to kings to do evil,
> For the throne is established by righteousness. (16.12)

[52] On the problems of the word *qesem* see H. Cazelles, *VT* 8, 1958, p. 324; Gemser, *op. cit., ad loc.*

(*c*) *The king as seen by the courtier.* We have already considered[53] the views of the two books on the courtier as counsellor. We may, however, conclude with a few proverbs which give expression to the character of the relationship of king and courtier as it is conceived in both books.

II Sam. 14.28-33, although it concerns the king's son and not a courtier, nevertheless gives a valuable insight into the importance of the right of access to the king; the importance of 'seeing the king's face' is expressed in very similar terms in Proverbs:

In the light of the king's face there is life,
And his favour is like the clouds which bring the spring rain. (16.15)

On the other hand, the fear of the king's wrath which provoked —for example—the suicide of Ahithophel is seen in such proverbs as 20.2:

> The dread wrath of a king is like the growling of a lion;
> He who provokes him to anger forfeits his life.

(Cf. also 19.12.)

Other themes. A few examples may be given of other themes which occur in both books.

(*a*) *Ambition.* This is a theme which runs through the whole of the Succession Narrative. Prov. 27.20, with its hint of a parallel between uncontrolled ambition and death, might well serve as an epitaph for Absalom and Adonijah, and—as applied to lust rather than ambition—for Amnon:

> Sheol and Abaddon are never satisfied,
> And never satisfied are the eyes of man.

(*b*) *Frustration and fulfilment.* When Amnon 'made himself ill' because of his inability to possess Tamar (II Sam. 13.2), he perfectly exemplified the first half of Prov. 13.12, which states that

> Hope deferred makes the heart sick;

though the second half, which states that

> A desire fulfilled is a tree of life

comes to a conclusion totally opposed to that implied in the story. But the observation that the continued frustration of one's

---

[53] Pp. 57ff., *supra.*

desires leads to physical sickness was well observed by both authors. It also occurs in the story of Naboth's Vineyard (I Kings 21.4).

(*c*) *Friendship, loyalty and treachery*. These interrelated themes run through almost every incident in the Succession Narrative, from David's kindness to Meribbaal for the sake of his friendship with Jonathan (II Sam. 9) to his and Solomon's treatment of Joab and Abiathar at the very end of the book. The author, by means of a multitude of examples, seems to pose above all the question of true friendship and loyalty, of which the touchstones are that they are unaffected either by personal danger or by thoughts of gain. The examples which he gives are mainly of two kinds: those concerned with David's behaviour to those who have a right to expect loyalty (*ḥesed*) from him (Uriah, Joab, Abiathar) and those which describe the behaviour of such people towards him (Uriah, Ittai, Ahithophel, Hushai, Joab).

The wisdom teachers did not neglect this important subject, and Proverbs contains a number of proverbs about it, of which some are directly illustrated in the Succession Narrative.

One proverb expresses the disillusionment of a man who has experienced constant betrayal by his friends:

Many a man proclaims his loyalty (*ḥesed*),
But a faithful man ('*îš* '*emūnîm*) who can find? (Prov. 20.6)

This is abundantly illustrated in the Succession Narrative, which abounds in protestations of loyalty, but also in betrayals. Both books thus provide us with a startlingly realistic picture of the intrigues of court life.

The protestation of loyalty mentioned in Prov. 20.6 was evidently a regular feature of the courtier's life: we find no less than five examples of it in the Succession Narrative, each in a form suited to the occasion:

'What is your servant, that you should look upon a dead dog such as I?' (Meribbaal to David, II Sam. 9.8)

'Behold, your servants are ready to do whatever my lord the king decides.' (David's servants to their master, 15.15)

'As Yahweh lives, and as my lord the king lives, wherever my lord the king shall be, whether for death or for life, there also will your servant be.' (Ittai to David, 15.21)

'I do obeisance; let me ever find favour in your sight, my lord the king.' (Ziba to David, 16.4)

'Whom Yahweh and this people and all the men of Israel have chosen, his will I be, and with him will I remain. And again, whom should I serve? Should it not be his son? As I have served your father, so I will serve you.' (Hushai to Absalom, 16.18f.)

Failures in loyalty (*ḥesed*) are, however, equally numerous: apart from the rebellions of Absalom and Amnon, and of all who followed them, and of Sheba and his followers, the Succession Narrative records the disloyalty of Meribbaal to David (or, alternatively, of Ziba to Meribbaal), of David to his servant Uriah, of Hushai to Absalom, of Ahithophel to David, of Joab who murders Amasa while kissing him and addressing him as 'my brother' ('*āḥī*, II Sam. 20.9). The author does, however, recognize that there are some men worthy to be called 'faithful men' ('*īš* '*emūnīm*): Joab and Hushai, in their loyalty to David, are the chief examples of such men.

In the story of Hushai the author raises a deeper question of which Proverbs takes no account, although it is the kind of problem which might have been expressed by two contrasting proverbs. Hushai is a loyal friend who risks his life for his friend David, yet he is also, in the service of that friend, a treacherous man who professes loyalty to Absalom in order to bring about his destruction. The ethical question is explicitly raised in Absalom's question to him: 'Is this your loyalty (*ḥesed*) to your friend?' (II Sam. 16.17). The author does not make it clear whether Hushai's conduct is to be regarded as admirable or reprehensible.

That the true test of friendship comes in time of adversity, illustrated in the Succession Narrative by Ittai's and Hushai's loyalty to David and by Ahithophel's desertion, is also stated in Proverbs:

> A friend loves at all times,
> And a brother is born for adversity. (17.17)

The word brother ('*āḥ*) here is probably to be taken, as in the examples from the Succession Narrative, as referring to a covenantal, rather than a physical relationship; and the second half of the verse means that friendship implies the sharing of adversity as well as of success.

Joab's rebuke of David in II Sam. 19.5-7, his murder of Amasa, and Hushai's betrayal of Absalom are all illustrations of Prov. 27.6:

> Faithful are the wounds of a friend;
> Profuse are the kisses of an enemy.

(*d*) *Revenge*. Absalom's fatal act of revenge for the rape of Tamar was not in accordance with the prudent counsel of the wisdom teachers, who believed that retribution for misdeeds would come of its own accord:

> Do not say, 'I will repay evil';
> Wait for Yahweh, and he will help you. (Prov. 20.22)

It is not the object of the foregoing comparison to prove that the Succession Narrative was consciously illustrating the teaching of the Book of Proverbs, or any part of it, in its present form. It is perhaps unlikely that any of the collections in Proverbs had reached its present form when the Succession Narrative was written. But the wisdom teachers were already at work in Israel in the time of David, and had already begun to form collections of their proverbial teaching. It is here contended that there is a sufficiently close resemblance between Proverbs and the incidents and situations of the Succession Narrative to show that the author of the latter was not merely a man who shared the general outlook of the wisdom teachers, but was himself a wisdom teacher in the sense that he set out deliberately to illustrate specific proverbial teaching for the benefit of the pupils and ex-pupils of the schools.

IV

THE POLITICAL NOVEL IN EGYPT AND ISRAEL

In the foregoing chapters the case for regarding the Succession Narrative as a combination of propagandist political novel and wisdom instruction in narrative form has been argued exclusively on the basis of Old Testament evidence. We now turn to external evidence, that is, to the question whether examples of this rather unusual combination of genres are to be found in earlier, non-Israelite, literature. A priori this would seem to be not improbable: however highly one may estimate the originality of the 'Solomonic enlightenment', it is hardly to be supposed that such a sophisticated work could have been composed without the existence of earlier models; and such models must inevitably be sought mainly outside Israel.

The influence of Egyptian culture on Israel at this period has already been referred to.[1] It is, indeed, being increasingly realized that Egyptian influence on Palestine at all periods has in the past been seriously underestimated. This is partly due to the fact that some early theories of such influence were sometimes put forward[2] with more enthusiasm than judgment, and this led to a reaction; but more recently both Egyptologists and biblical scholars have been building a more solid foundation for it.[3] It is now clearly recognized that significant cultural contacts between Canaan and Egypt began long before the time of David, during the long period of Egyptian domination in the second millennium BC.[4] The visits of Egyptian sailors to Phoenician ports may have been the means by which some motifs of Egyptian folk-lore reached Syria and Palestine,[5]

[1] Pp. 3ff., supra.
[2] E.g. by J. H. Breasted, The Dawn of Conscience, New York, 1934.
[3] See especially S. Morenz, 'Die ägyptische Literatur und die Umwelt' (Handbuch der Orientalistik I 2, pp. 194-206), for a survey.
[4] S. Morenz, 'Ägyptologische Beiträge zur Erforschung der Weisheitsliteratur Israels' (Les sagesses du proche orient ancien, pp. 65ff.).
[5] G. Lefebvre, Romans et contes égyptiens de l'époque pharaonique, Paris, 1949, pp. xii ff.

and by which also Syrian deities became known in Egypt. But it is probable that the bulk of literary influences were transmitted at the level of the court. There is evidence that the courts of Canaanite vassal kings were influenced culturally as well as administratively by the dominating power.[6] Such influences will thus have reached Israel by two routes: indirectly through the adoption by David and Solomon of Canaanite manners and customs, and directly through Israel's political contacts with the Egyptian court.[7]

There are today strong indications that a wide range of Old Testament literature shows Egyptian influence.[8] The Egyptologist Raymond Weill, while pointing out that the subject as a whole has never been thoroughly investigated, and calling for the application—but more systematically—to other genres of the method which Humbert[9] had applied to the wisdom literature, was nevertheless able to give numerous examples which have already come to light.[10]

Until recently it had been assumed that inability to read Egyptian literature would have hindered its influence on Israelite writers. But as far as the Israelite court is concerned this argument would appear to be mistaken. Weill's claim that 'we can clearly see today that the biblical writers had at their disposal the entire range of Egyptian literature' may be an exaggeration, but we cannot dismiss the considered opinion of S. Morenz, who claims that the presence at Solomon's court of bilingual officials with a competent knowledge of Egyptian writing must be regarded, in view of what we now know of that court and its diplomatic relations with Egypt, as absolutely beyond question[11]; and what is true of Solomon's court may reasonably be supposed to be true of David's also.

As has already been stated,[12] we must include narrative litera-

---

[6] E.g. the statement of Zakar-Baal, prince of Byblos, in the *Journey of Wenamon*, that the skill and learning of his people had been derived from Egypt (*ANET*, p. 27).

[7] Solomon's marriage to the daughter of Pharaoh (I Kings 3.1) and Pharaoh's gift to Solomon of the city of Gezer (I Kings 9.16) prove the existence of such contacts.

[8] Morenz, *art. cit.* in *Handbuch der Orientalistik*.   [9] *Op. cit.*

[10] R. Weill, 'Les transmissions littéraires d'Egypte à Israël', *Revue d'Egyptologie, cahier complémentaire* (I), Cairo, 1950, pp. 43-61.

[11] *Art. cit.* in *Handbuch der Orientalistik*.

[12] Pp. 6ff., 76ff., *supra*.

ture among the literary genres affected. Lefebvre[13] drew attention to the existence of common themes and traits in Egyptian
and Israelite storytelling[14]; but it is more to the point for the
present purpose to consider the influence of the Egyptian *historical novel*.[15]

1. *The 'royal novel' in Egypt*

The most characteristic type of Egyptian historical novel is
that which has been called the 'royal novel' (*Königsnovelle*),[16] a
genre which persisted through most of Egyptian history down to
very late times. Its purpose was to commemorate some action of
a particular king which was believed to be of unusual importance
for the maintenance or strengthening of the world order and thus
—the two things were not distinguished in Egyptian thought—
of the Egyptian state. Such actions included the renovation of
ancient temples and the building of new ones, the completion of
the building work of predecessors, the revival or institution of
cults, foreign conquests, the quelling of rebellions, etc. These
'royal novels' contributed to the glorification of kingship, and
of the dynasty in particular, and were often inscribed on the walls
of temples or other buildings, but were also copied on papyrus
and read as literature.

[13] *Op. cit.*, pp. x-xxv.

[14] The similarity between the Joseph Narrative and the Egyptian *Tale of
Two Brothers* (*ANET*, pp. 23-25) is the best known example. But Lefebvre
gives other examples, of which the most striking is the similarity between
the *Tale of Horus and Seth* (translation in Lefebvre; this section is not given
in *ANET*) and the Parable of Nathan in II Sam. 12.1ff., where in both cases
a fictitious tale about an act of injustice is told in order to lead the judge to
convict himself. The parallel between Nathan's 'You are the man!' and Isis'
'Weep for yourself! Your own mouth has declared it; your own cleverness
has condemned you!' is a striking one.

[15] This is not the place to discuss the assertion which has been made, e.g.
by von Rad ('Beginnings', p. 167), that the Egyptians had no true concept
of history and were thus incapable of historiography; but it may be pointed
out that this opinion has been challenged by a number of scholars, including
A. Hermann (*Die ägyptische Königsnovelle*, Leipzig, 1938) and R. de Vaux
('Jérusalem et les prophètes', *RB* 73, 1966, p. 485).

[16] A. Hermann, *op. cit.*; S. Herrmann, 'Die Königsnovelle in Ägypten
und Israel' (*Wissenschaftliche Zeitschrift Universitäts Leipzig* 3, 1953-1954,
Gesellschafts- und Sprachwissenschaftliche Reihe—Heft 1, Leipzig, pp. 51-62).
The translation 'royal novel' is used here for convenience. It is not an
accurate translation of *Königsnovelle*, but is perhaps to be preferred to D. R.
Ap-Thomas' 'King's Letter', in his translation of M. Noth's 'David and
Israel in II Samuel VII', in *The Laws of the Pentateuch*, pp. 257f.

The setting of the royal novel is the court, and the emphasis on strict court ceremonial which is characteristic of it shows that the court was the milieu in which it was composed. The features characteristic of the genre are the king's revelation of his plan to the courtiers at the council-meeting, the courtiers' praise of the king's wisdom, and an account of how the plan was subsequently carried out. These features are not all invariably present, however, and others frequently appear in their place or in addition to them. A very frequent feature is the dream: the king recounts a dream in which the god has appeared to him and commanded or encouraged him to perform the deed in question. Other features which are sometimes included are a hymn of praise to the god Rē, a reference to Rē as the 'father' of the king, a statement that the king was chosen even before his birth to perform this action, an assertion that this divine choice confers legitimacy on the dynasty, and the offering of sacrifices and prayers. There is thus considerable flexibility and variation in form and contents, but whatever features may be absent or present, the royal novel always remains a recognizable literary genre.

Two variations are of particular interest. In some cases—especially in the *Bentresch Stele* from the Persian period—the royal novel is used as an excuse for telling an entertaining story: the literary imagination of the novelist has broken through the formal structure of the genre. In others—particularly the story of *Kamose's Delivery of Egypt from the Hyksos*[17]—it is a concern for historical accuracy which has caused a variation in the normal structure: when King Kamose has revealed to the courtiers his plan for defeating the Hyksos, the courtiers, instead of agreeing with the plan in the usual way, oppose it. But the king wins the argument, and then goes on to conduct a successful and crucially important campaign.

It is important to notice that, in spite of the formal character of the royal novel and its practical purpose of recording great deeds to the glory of the king, the writers—even where they did not depart from the formal structure—seized every opportunity to make it a literature of entertainment. Although in most cases there was little attempt at serious portrayal of character, the royal novel was far from being a purely stylized composition, and was intended from the first for a reading public. Her-

17 *ANET*, pp. 232f.

mann[18] regarded it as the ancestor of the modern short story.

2. The 'royal novel' in the Old Testament

It has been clearly demonstrated by a number of scholars[19] that there are a number of passages in the narrative books of the Old Testament which so closely resemble the Egyptian royal novel that their dependence on it is beyond doubt. All these passages are concerned, like their Egyptian models, with the achievements and glory of the king and the legitimacy and greatness of the dynasty.

Perhaps the clearest case is *I Kings* 3.1-15. Here the divine revelation made to the king in a dream at the holy place followed by his return to the capital and offering of sacrifice exactly follows the sequence of events in the *Sphinx Stele* of Tutmose IV,[20] and many of the details also correspond, especially the contents of Solomon's address to God in the dream, with its reference to the origin of the dynasty in a divine appointment. Some of the words attributed to Solomon, especially 'I am but a little child; I do not know how to go out or come in' (v. 7) are almost identical with phrases in another Egyptian royal novel, the *Karnak Inscription* of Tutmose III.[21] The purpose in all three cases, as S. Herrmann observed, is to strengthen the belief in the legitimacy of the dynasty by a doctrine of predestination—a matter of political necessity for Solomon, as we have seen.

II Samuel 7, the 'foundation document of David's dynasty',[22] with its ceremonial beginning—'the king sitting in his palace', v. 1—its preoccupation both with the building of a temple and the establishment of the dynasty, the night vision and the agreement of the counsellor, Nathan, with the king's plan,[23] also corresponds both in general plan and in many details to a number of Egyptian royal novels.[24] Admittedly some drastic innovations

[18] *Op. cit.*, p. 36.
[19] Especially A. Hermann and S. Herrmann. The thesis has been accepted by E. Otto, 'Geschichtliche Literatur: Annalistik und Königsnovelle' (*Handbuch der Orientalistik* I 2, p. 144); M. Noth, 'David and Israel in II Samuel VII' and M. Noth, *Könige*, p. 46; de Vaux, 'Jérusalem et les prophètes', pp. 484ff.
[20] *ANET*, p. 449.   [21] Not in *ANET*.
[22] S. Herrmann, *art. cit.*, pp. 57-61.
[23] The opposition of Yahweh to the plan constitutes a variation. This novel combines the usual feature of the courtiers' assent to the king's plan with the less frequent one of opposition to it!
[24] So A. Hermann, S. Herrmann, Noth and de Vaux.

have been made, of which the greatest is that the king is no longer
the central figure: this place is now taken by Yahweh. But, as
S. Herrmann pointed out in this connexion, the genre is a very
flexible one, and the Egyptian novelists took almost as much
liberty with it as does the author of II Sam. 7. Allowing for the
very special Israelite circumstances, especially religious ones, for
which the genre had to be adapted, this story departs remarkably
little from the traditional form.

A. Hermann suggested[25] that the royal novel form is also to be
found in the account of Solomon's building of the Temple (I King's
5.1-8.66) and in Solomon's second dream in I Kings 9. It must
be admitted that some characteristic themes of the royal novel,
especially the divine command to build a temple (5.5; 8.19), the
royal plan and its execution, the hymn, prayer and making of
offerings, the divine legitimization of the dynasty and the dream
all occur there.[26] If this view is accepted, we are then confronted
with the remarkable fact that more than half of the history of
Solomon's reign (I Kings 3-11) shows the influence, in varying
degrees, of the royal novel, the remainder consisting mainly of
annalistic material and later theological additions. Such influence
is found nowhere else in the Old Testament except in II Sam. 7:
in other words, all these passages show that the Israelite historians and theologians of this period of Israelite history found
in earlier Egyptian literature analogies with their own dynastic
and theological preoccupations.

3. *The Egyptian novel and the Succession Narrative*

The fact that the Egyptian literary genre of the royal novel
was known to the early historians of Israel and was applied by
them to the history of Solomon's reign has implications for our
enquiry into possible literary models for the Succession Narrative.
The latter is obviously not itself a royal novel in the Egyptian
sense: it corresponds with it neither in form nor in contents, and
it is much longer. Nevertheless there are similarities of theme and
purpose: in both the king is the central figure, and the normal
setting is the court, in which the king is surrounded by his ad-

[25] *Op. cit.*, p. 39.
[26] Compare especially the *Dedicatory Inscription of Sesostris I* in Erman,
op. cit., pp. 49-52.

visers; while the episode of Absalom's rebellion, when the king leaves the court and takes charge of a military operation, corresponds to the accounts of quelling of rebels which occur in some of the Egyptian royal novels. The numerous individual court scenes, although in structure they do not correspond very closely to the royal novel, nevertheless closely resemble it in general atmosphere and in some of the details of court ceremonial. This not only confirms the view that Israelite royal ceremonial was at least partly modelled on Egyptian, but also suggests literary influence in the way in which court life was described.

To compare the Succession Narrative in this general way with the royal novel is, however, to confine the enquiry to too narrow a field. The Egyptian political or historical novel was not confined to the genre of the royal novel, nor were descriptions of court life confined to it. Egyptian literature offers a wide range of such literature. Many stories are no more than fairy stories or popular tales[27]; but from at least the beginning of the Middle Kingdom we have examples of more sophisticated novels written for an educated public, sometimes with a political motive, but even so with the object of entertaining the reader, not with crude accounts of the supernatural, as in the popular tales, but with wit and humour, atmosphere, characterization and psychological insight and elegant style.[28] Among the most outstanding examples are the *Story of Sinuhe*,[29] written probably in the nineteenth century BC, and the *Journey of Wenamon*,[30] written about 1100 BC.

Novels such as these bear no specific resemblance to the Succession Narrative as far as their contents are concerned; but as notable examples of the art of the novel they were well known, at least among the educated classes of Egypt, at the time when its author was writing. In particular, the *Story of Sinuhe* was so popular that MSS of it are extant from every period from the eighteenth to the tenth century, and Gardiner said of it that 'to the young scribes of the eighteenth and nineteenth dynasties' (i.e. from about the sixteenth to the thirteenth century BC) 'the ad-

---

[27] See Lefebvre, *op. cit.*, for translations and introductions.
[28] Lefebvre, *op. cit.*, pp. viff.; T. E. Peet, *A Comparative Study of the Literature of Egypt, Palestine and Mesopotamia (Schweich Lectures*, 1929), London, 1931, pp. 27-47; G. Roeder, *Altägyptische Erzählungen und Märchen*, Jena, 1927, pp. XIff.
[29] Erman, *op. cit.*, pp. 14-29; *ANET*, pp. 18-22; cf. Peet, *op. cit.*, pp. 33-38.
[30] Erman, pp. 174-185; *ANET*, pp. 25-29; cf. Peet, pp. 47-50.

ventures of Sinuhe were doubtless as familiar as those of Robinson Crusoe to the English child'.[31]

This being so, it is of some importance that these Egyptian novels, like the Succession Narrative, were greatly influenced by didactic—that is, proverbial—wisdom literature, and that indeed they finally achieved a fusion of the two genres.[32] Even in the relatively unsophisticated *Story of the Shipwrecked Sailor*[33] from the Middle Kingdom, one of the characters quotes from the Old Kingdom *Instruction of Ptahhotep* in giving good advice to the sailor.[34] The early Middle Kingdom *Complaints of the Eloquent Peasant*,[35] written apparently by a learned scribe to show off his accomplishments, goes a step further: it is 'a piece of wisdom-literature with a story for setting',[36] a type of literature which became very popular in later times.[37] It abounds in quotations from a wide range of earlier literature including proverbial literature, and one of its aims is to exemplify all the virtues and vices with which the wisdom literature deals,[38] while the story itself is concerned with the theme of social justice as the basis on which the world order rests.

It is, however, the *Story of Sinuhe* which represents the fullest achievement in this field.[39] The story is told in the autobiographical style of the Egyptian tomb-inscriptions. Sinuhe, an official of high rank attendant upon the Crown Princess, recounts the story of his life. The narrative begins with the death of the king, Amenemhet I. Hearing of this event by chance when he is absent from the capital, and suspecting from his knowledge of the political situation that there would be a struggle for the succession which would put his life in danger, Sinuhe fled on an impulse eastwards across the frontier into the 'land of Retenu',

---

[31] A. H. Gardiner, *Notes on the Story of Sinuhe*, Paris, p. 164.
[32] Peet, *op. cit.*, pp. 40f.
[33] Erman, pp. 29 35; cf. Peet, pp. 28-32.
[34] J. Spiegel, 'Göttergeschichten, Erzählungen, Märchen, Fabeln' (*Handbuch der Orientalistik* I 2, p. 123).
[35] Erman, pp. 116-131; *ANET*, pp. 407-410; cf. Peet, pp. 38-40.
[36] Peet, p. 41.
[37] E.g. the *Words of Ahiqar*; the *Book of Tobit*.
[38] E. Suys, *Etude sur le conte du fellah plaideur* (An. Or. 5), Rome, 1933, pp. xxiv-xxvii.
[39] See the studies by Lefebvre (pp. vif.), Peet (pp. 34-36), Spiegel (*Handbuch der Orientalistik* I 2, p. 123), Gardiner (*Sinuhe*, pp. 164-168), Roeder (p. XI) and G. Posener, *Littérature et politique dans l'Egypte de la 12ᵉ dynastie*, Paris, 1956, pp. 87-115.

i.e. Syria. There he was treated kindly, and eventually settled in Upper Retenu (Palestine) and became a wealthy and influential chieftain. But as he grew old he began to pine for his homeland and especially to grieve that he would be denied a proper burial according to Egyptian customs.

A report of his plight was made to the king of Egypt, now Sesostris I, the king who had succeeded his father Amenemhet at the beginning of the story, and a free pardon was agreed upon. Sesostris sent Sinuhe a letter urging him to return home. He did so, and on arrival was treated most honourably and restored to his former high rank with the certain expectation, so important to the Egyptians, of a magnificent burial. The story ends with Sinuhe aged but content to die, all his desires having been fulfilled.

This story, which, as we have seen, became and remained a classic for many centuries, has, in spite of the dissimilarity of the subject, many of the features which we observed in the Succession Narrative. It is a historical novel of great entertainment value, based loosely on historical events; it deals, not with a remote period of the past, but with the period immediately preceding the time when it was written, and so reflects contemporary life; unlike most Egyptian stories it makes no use of supernatural interventions but tells an entirely credible story in which the characters behave at all times in a rational manner; it is not content to tell a tale, but is a psychological study which probes the motives of the characters; it shows great skill in the selection, shaping and arrangement of a small number of effective scenes, which are described in an extremely vivid manner; it aspires to elegance of style and diction; and it displays[40] the same curiosity about the world, and confidence in the civilized order inaugurated by the newly established dynasty[41] which were also characteristic, so many centuries later, of the age of David and Solomon.

In addition to these characteristics the *Story of Sinuhe* shows the influence of the wisdom literature.[42] There are few, if any, actual quotations from earlier proverbial literature, but the psychological element in the story is clearly dependent on the ideals and admonitions which the wisdom literature had brought

---

[40] Spiegel, *art. cit.*, pp. 131f.
[41] Amenemhet I was the founder of the Twelfth Dynasty.
[42] Peet, p. 41.

to the fore. The story begins and ends in the royal court; and although most of Sinuhe's life was spent in exile, his thoughts constantly turned to the court, in which he had been brought up.[43] The book expresses the ideal of Egyptian life as seen from the point of view of the courtier: in spite of the dangers of life at court, to be forced to live away from it, even in circumstances of wealth and power, is misery. Much of the book is concerned with the person of the king, who is depicted in terms familiar from the wisdom literature, as fearsome, yet capable of great beneficence: the source of life and death. The arts of the courtier —humility before the king, caution in speech, good counsel and prudent silence—are well illustrated. The themes of wealth, filial piety—exemplified by Sesostris—old age and a good burial are all dwelt upon. Finally the central character, Sinuhe himself, is presented—like the characters in the Succession Narrative—as a mixture of wisdom and folly, both a warning and an example. He is punished, by his prolonged exile, for the folly of running away, as he says, 'when no one had run after me'[44]; but when he comes to his senses and regrets his folly, he is restored to favour and good fortune.

4. *Political aspects of Egyptian and Israelite literature*

One similarity between the *Story of Sinuhe* and the Succession Narrative remains to be mentioned. This is the fact that both are *political* novels. In order to explain the full significance of this it is necessary to consider in some detail the political situation which the *Story of Sinuhe* reflects.[45]

Amenemhet I, the king whose death was the occasion for the flight of Sinuhe, was the founder of the Twelfth Dynasty, and also has a good claim to be considered as the founder of that period of high civilization in Egypt which is known as the Middle Kingdom. The previous two centuries, after the collapse of the Old Kingdom, had been a period of political and economic chaos and of warfare between rival feudal families. In the absence of

[43] See Brunner, *Erziehung*, p. 16, n. 23. On the part played by scribes as both authors and transmitters of these stories see Brunner, *Erziehung*, p. 101; Roeder, *op. cit.*, p. XV; Suys, *op. cit.*, pp. xxivf.

[44] Cf. Prov. 28.1a: 'The wicked flee when no one pursues.'

[45] Here I follow especially Posener, *op. cit.*, pp. 1-20. But the outlines of the events are given in most surveys of Egyptian history, e.g. C. Aldred, *The Egyptians* (Ancient People and Places), London, 1961, pp. 118-122.

political unity, the standards of both material and cultural life had seriously declined. The political reunification of the country had begun under the kings of the Eleventh Dynasty; but it was only under Amenemhet I that law and order returned to Egypt under a strong ruler. Amenemhet was therefore regarded by later generations as one of the great figures of Egyptian history.

After he had obtained the throne, Amenemhet found himself obliged to turn his attention to three pressing tasks: it was necessary to secure the dynasty and to ensure that the supporters of the previous dynasty were rendered incapable of a return to power; to restore general confidence in, and respect for, the monarchy itself as an institution, after a period in which it had been brought into contempt; and to restore the system of orderly administration of the country which had broken down.

In pursuance of these objectives Amenemhet moved the capital from Thebes to the north, and made Amon the principal god in place of Montu, who had been favoured by the previous dynasty. He wished to make it clear that a new beginning had been made, and that the past was to be forgotten. But at the same time he pursued a policy of conciliation towards the supporters of Montu, whose worship was allowed to continue. He also took measures to restore and replenish the profession of scribes, which had become seriously depleted, but without which it was impossible to administer the country efficiently.

Although Amenemhet's policies were in the main successful, he did not live to see the fruits of his work, but was murdered in a palace conspiracy in which it is probable that some of his own sons were implicated.[46] Sinuhe's statement that he fled on hearing the news of the king's death is an allusion to the circumstances— dangerous for all those who were close to the king or the royal princes—of his death, and to the uncertainty about the succession. In the event it was the king's son Sesostris I who succeeded: he is the king who many years later sent for Sinuhe and restored him to favour.

Sesostris I's reign was a long and successful one. But, like his

---

[46] The details of the conspiracy are obscure; but Posener (*op. cit.*, p. 82) concludes from the dead king's complaint in the *Instruction of Amenemhet* that 'he who partook of my food, he to whom I had held out my arms took advantage of me', together with the rather obscure account of the king's death at the beginning of the *Story of Sinuhe*, that some of the king's sons were involved.

father, though for somewhat different reasons, he was at first faced with grave dangers, especially from those who disputed his right to the throne. However, he overcame these difficulties and went on to restore Egypt to a state of great prosperity. His own dynasty lasted altogether for some 200 years, and the Middle Kingdom endured until the Hyksos conquest some 350 years after the accession of Amenemhet I.

One of the chief means used by both Amenemhet and Sesostris to secure their position and to achieve their political and administrative aims was political propaganda in the form of literary works of various kinds. At least five such works have survived.

The *Prophecy of Neferty*[47] is a work composed in the form of a royal novel, but its chief feature is a lengthy prophecy supposed to have been pronounced by one Neferty. The setting is a 'golden age' of the past: the reign of King Snefru (Fourth Dynasty). At the king's request to be entertained by someone who is able to speak 'a few fine words or choice speeches', Neferty, a lector-priest of the goddess Bastet, utters a prophecy. The present age of prosperity will be succeeded by a time of troubles for Egypt; but afterwards there will appear a king named Ameny, who will overcome Egypt's enemies and restore the golden age, re-establishing justice and prosperity. There is no doubt that this book is a work of propaganda commissioned by the government of Amenemhet I, early in his reign, to justify his occupation of the throne and to rally support for his policies. 'Ameny' is another name of Amenemhet, and the time of troubles which, according to the prophecy, will precede his accession is that period of decline between the Old and Middle Kingdoms known as the First Intermediate Period. The author skilfully exploits the fears and hopes of his contemporaries, interpreting the early achievements of Amenemhet as only the prelude to even greater benefits which this 'messianic' king will confer on the nation.

Two other works, the *Kemit*[48] and the *Satire on the Trades*,[49] addressed themselves to the problem of reviving and re-establishing the scribal profession: the latter paints a rosy picture of the

---

[47] The name 'Neferty' was formerly thought to be 'Neferrohu'. Translations in Erman, pp. 110-115; *ANET*, pp. 444-446. There is a full description and discussion in Posener, *op. cit.*, pp. 21-60.

[48] On this work see Brunner, *Erziehung*, pp. 14f., and *ibid.*, pp. 158f. (Qu. X) for a short extract.

[49] Erman, pp. 67-72; *ANET*, pp. 432-434.

advantages of being a scribe, while the former sets out the principles of scribal education.

A fourth work is the *Instruction of Amenemhet*,[50] written by Khety, the author of the *Satire on the Trades*.[51] It was composed after the death of Amenemhet and the accession of Sesostris I, and purports to be the political testament of Amenemhet, containing the advice which the old king gave to his son. It was not the first work of this kind: the *Instruction for Merikare*, attributed to a king of one of the rival dynasties of the First Intermediate Period, some 200 years before, is an earlier example of the same genre. The *Instruction of Amenemhet* is at the same time an apologia for Amenemhet himself, and a justification of his son's claim to the throne.[52]

Finally, the *Story of Sinuhe*, already described, must be regarded as belonging to the same group of works, although there are some important differences. It was evidently written some time after the accession of Sesostris, when the king was already firmly settled on his throne, with both the succession and the dynasty firmly established; and it is apparently not a commissioned work but a voluntary tribute to the greatness and beneficence of Sesostris by one who sincerely admired him. Nevertheless it is a political novel in the sense that it was directly inspired by, and also greatly contributed to, the popularity of the dynasty.

The history of the early years of the Twelfth Dynasty and the literature which they inspired have been dealt with at some length because of the existence of a remarkable number of points of similarity between this 'age of enlightenment' in Egypt in the twentieth century BC and that of Israel in the tenth. The following are some of the more important circumstances which are common to both:

1. A new dynasty was founded by a strong king after a period of chaos and political disunity (Amenemhet I; David).

2. The establishment of the dynasty was marked, for political reasons, by a change of capital and by religious innovations (Amenemhet's adoption of Amon and moving of the capital to

---

[50] Erman, pp. 72-74; *ANET*, pp. 418f. See also Posener, *op. cit.*, pp. 61-86.

[51] The identification is made in the Chester Beatty Papyrus IV, edited by A. H. Gardiner in *Hieratic Papyri in the British Museum, Third Series*, London, 1935.

[52] This work is considered in greater detail on pp. 110ff., *infra*.

the north; David's choice of Jerusalem and transfer of the Ark there).

3. The new dynasty was at first hampered by the lack of an adequate scribal class which was, however, quickly established (Amenemhet's encouragement of the scribal profession; David's importation of foreign scribes).

4. The new dynasty supported its claim to the throne by means of prophecy (*Prophecy of Neferty*; the prophecy of Nathan in II Sam. 7).

5. The achievements of the founder were in each case handed on to his successor, though not without difficulty.

6. The reign of the founder was marked in each case, especially towards the end, by intrigues and rebellions in which his sons were implicated.

7. Both periods were marked by a remarkable burst of literary activity unsurpassed in any other comparable period in the history of the nation. This literature included:

(*a*) Prophetic testimonies to the divine election of the founder.

(*b*) Educational and wisdom literature (*Kemit, Satire on the Trades, Instruction of Amenemhet*; early collections in Proverbs, references to Solomon's wisdom in I Kings). Some of this is specifically *royal* wisdom (*Amenemhet*; tradition of Solomonic literary activity).

(*c*) True or fictitious political testaments in the form of final instructions from founder to successor (*Amenemhet*; I Kings 2.1-9).

(*d*) Political novels which include an account of the troubles which preceded and accompanied the accession of the successor, and which also combine psychological and literary interests with wisdom (*Sinuhe*; Succession Narrative).

(*e*) Royal novels extolling the claims or achievements of the régime in more formal terms (*Dedicatory Inscription of Sesostris I*, giving an account of that ruler's building of a temple at Heliopolis; royal novels in I Kings, including the account of Solomon's building of the Temple at Jerusalem).

Since we know that the Egyptian literature of this period continued to be copied and read for many centuries afterwards,[53]

[53] See H. Kees, 'Die ägyptische Literatur' (*Handbuch der Orientalistik* I 2, pp. 3-21).

and since we have positive evidence of Egyptian literary influence
in the case of the royal novel, it is not unreasonable to suppose
that some of the similarities between the themes of the other
literary products of the two periods in question should be due to
more than mere coincidence. The Egyptian literature of the
early twelfth Dynasty, when the prestige of the monarchy was
restored, is also the only Egyptian literature which presents kings
as human beings and discusses, rather than merely extols, the
nature of monarchy and the problems with which it has to deal.[54]
What more natural than that the scribes of David and Solomon,
faced with problems so similar to those discussed in this earlier
Egyptian literature, should have been inspired by it as they
wrote their works of propaganda?

It would be possible to pursue this question by more detailed
comparison of any of the types of literature referred to above.
Here we are concerned with the literary influences which may
have helped to inspire the author of the Succession Narrative.
This question may best be pursued by a detailed comparison of
the Succession Narrative with the *Instruction of Amenemhet*.

5. *The Succession Narrative and the Instruction of Amenemhet*

The *Instruction of Amenemhet* is ostensibly a wisdom instruction
containing advice given by Amenemhet I to his successor; but
the authorship is fictitious. The work was written in the reign of
Sesostris I, and its primary aim is political.[55] More than half of
the work is narrative: the old king describes, in somewhat veiled
terms, the successful attack on his life, and also describes his
achievements, in a mixture of the well known autobiographical
style found in tomb inscriptions and of straightforward narrative.
He also confirms Sesostris as his successor:

[54] Posener, *op. cit.*, pp. 141ff.

[55] So A. de Buck, 'The Instruction of Amenemmes' (*Mélanges Maspéro* I 2,
Cairo, 1935-38, pp. 847-852); 'La composition littéraire des enseignements
d'Amenemhat', *Muséon* 59, 1946, pp. 183-200. Also Posener, *op. cit.*, pp. 67ff.;
E. Otto, 'Weltanschauliche und politische Tendenzschriften' (*Handbuch der
Orientalistik* I 2, pp. 117f.). A. H. Gardiner, in 'The Earliest Manuscripts of
the Instruction of Amenemmes I' (*Mélanges Maspéro* I 2, pp. 479-496), maintained that the attack on the king's life referred to in the book was an unsuccessful one, and that it is a genuine instruction composed by that king
during his lifetime. This opinion has not been generally accepted. See
B. Gunn, *JEA* 27, 1941, pp. 2-5 on the interpretation of the phrase 'message
of truth' as meaning 'dream'—implying that Amenemhet is here represented
as bringing a message from the grave.

'Hearken to what I have to say to thee, that thou mayest be king of the land and ruler of the regions.'

'Thou art my own heart; my eyes behold thee.'

At first sight, *Amenemhet* seems to be in every way a totally different kind of work from the Succession Narrative: it is short, it is autobiographical, it is not a novel, it makes no psychological study of character, it does not express wisdom teaching through narrative, but simply sets the two genres side by side. There is no question of imitation of style or of literary structure, although both works have been highly praised as literature,[56] and both represent attempts to burst the traditional bonds of wisdom literature and to create a fresh genre by combining existing literary types.

Yet in spite of the great differences between the two works, they have a great deal in common.

1. *Authorship*. The author of *Amenemhet* was, as is shown by the fact that he was also the author of the *Satire on the Trades*, a scribe and a wisdom teacher. We see in him, as in the author of the Succession Narrative, a man who combined the roles of educator, administrator and political propagandist.

2. *The situation*. The historical situations in which the two books were written were—apart from the fact that Amenemhet, unlike David, did not die a natural death—exactly identical: both were written early in the reign of the second king of a new dynasty after a political crisis concerning the succession, and when the position of the new king was not yet secure.

3. *Aims*. It is interesting to note that in both cases the main political aim is undisputed, while the somewhat ambiguous treatment of the main character (Amenemhet, David) makes an assessment of the secondary political aims more difficult. In both cases it is quite clear that the author's main intention is to justify the position and claim of the new king as the rightful successor, designated by his predecessor.[57] But Amenemhet is presented as a king who, in spite of his greatness and his achievements, made

---

[56] For *Amenemhet* see de Buck, 'Composition littéraire', p. 200; Posener, *op. cit.*, p. 144.

[57] De Buck, Posener and Otto agree on this. Even Gardiner, who believed that the book was written by Amenemhet himself, was of the same opinion.

mistakes, against which he now warns his son. Vandier[58] believed that the 'confession' of Amenemhet that the weakness of his internal policy was the cause of his overthrow and murder was intended to justify Sesostris' introduction of a new and firmer policy. If this is so, it would correspond exactly to David's counsel, in his political testament, to Solomon to be ruthless in getting rid of potential enemies (I Kings 2.5-9).

4. *The political testament.* *Amenemhet* is in its entirety the fictitious political testament of Amenemhet; strictly speaking the political testament of David occupies only a small part of the Succession Narrative. But in a larger sense the whole of the Succession Narrative may be so called. The whole of that work was needed to justify the claim of Solomon to be the rightful successor to the throne. In *Amenemhet*, it was apparently sufficient to represent the old king as confirming the succession in a brief statement; the Succession Narrative introduces a similar statement (I Kings 1.29f.) as the climax of a long narrative which is expressed, not in the first person as an autobiography in the Egyptian style, a style to which the Israelites were not accustomed, but in the third person style which was characteristic of Israelite narrative literature. Yet this narrative has precisely the same function as the corresponding statements in *Amenemhet*.

5. *The justification of the régime.* *Amenemhet* devotes much space to a description, in the first person, of the achievements of the old king. This was extremely germane to the author's purpose: merely to show that Sesostris' claim to be the rightful successor, designated by his father, would have been useless apart from a justification of the régime itself: that is, of the dynasty. Unless Amenemhet had himself justified his own usurpation of the throne and the supplanting of his rivals by pointing to his achievements as king, the legitimacy of Sesostris as his heir would still not prove his right to be king. The questions of the dynasty and the succession were inseparably bound up together. In the Succession Narrative there is no comparable account of David's military, political and administrative achievements because this was not necessary: it had been done elsewhere. But some justification of the régime itself was called for, as in *Amenem-*

---

[58] Cited by Posener (*op. cit.*, p. 86), who considers this view to be a possibility.

het; and this is certainly one of the motives of the Succession Narrative, as the three passages referring to Yahweh's hidden purpose regarding the régime, already referred to,[59] clearly show.

6. *The characterization of the king.* The figure of Amenemhet, as presented in the *Instruction*, is 'the most human portrait of the Pharaoh in the whole of Egyptian literature'.[60] It was no doubt the historical circumstances and the social and literary tendencies of the age, especially as manifested in the wisdom literature, which were responsible for this 'humanization' of the king. The fact remains that the portrait is unique, neither anticipated in the earlier literature nor repeated; although the portrait of the royal family in *Sinuhe*, written a few years later, approaches it to some extent. But even in *Sinuhe* there is no suggestion that the king, though affable, was capable of error or weakness. In *Amenemhet* the king is represented as a deeply disappointed and disillusioned man, betrayed by those whom he trusted and conscious that he is guilty of serious error in being too trustful, and in failing to detect the conspiracy against him until it was too late. He also admits to weariness, and even to a moment of weakness when the attack was made on him: 'there is no one valiant at night'.

The portrait of David in the Succession Narrative differs from this immensely in detail, since the circumstances were different; but it remains remarkably similar in its presentation of the king as in many respects an ordinary human being, who also knows moments of weakness and disillusionment.[61]

7. *The influence of wisdom literature. Amenemhet*, although its main aim is political, is also a genuine wisdom instruction in its own right.[62] It has much in common with earlier instructions: the exhortation to 'hearken what I have to say to thee' reminds us of *Ptahhotep*, and the general tone is not unlike the *Instruction for Merikare*, written some 200 years earlier. But chiefly the author makes use of proverbs. These are easily distinguishable by their brevity, and by the fact that they are very similar to proverbs found in the other literatures of the ancient near East:

Hold thyself apart from those subordinate to thee . . . approach them not in thy loneliness.

[59] Pp. 52, 64ff., *supra*.   [60] Posener, *op. cit.*, p. 65.
[61] On the foregoing paragraphs see Posener, *op. cit.*, p. 65.
[62] De Buck, 'Composition littéraire', p. 192; Brunner, 'Die Weisheits-literatur'.

Fill not thy heart with a brother, nor know a friend.

Create not for thyself intimates—there is no fulfilment thereby.

No man has adherents in the day of distress.

One fights in the arena forgetful of yesterday. (I.e., men fail to learn from their mistakes.)

There is no fulfilment of happiness for him who does not know what he should know. (I.e., the ignorant come to grief.)

There is no one valiant at night, and there is no fighting alone.

No success may occur without a protector.

As befits a wisdom instruction, these proverbial statements are not, as in the Succession Narrative, used as the basis for the creation of narrative episodes, but stand in the text in their original form. But they are entirely appropriate to the disillusioned mood of the narrative passages, which constitute the bulk of the work, and form a unity with them so that the whole is informed by them. There is, however, one clear example of a proverb which has been transformed into narrative form:

It was he who ate my food that raised troops against me,
And he to whom I had held out my arms that took advantage of me.

Here the style, with its parallelism, corresponds to the proverb, but the tense and the context show that this is narrative, and not a general statement.

So, as in the Succession Narrative, the central character of *Amenemhet* serves as an example of proverbial wisdom. The only difference is that the narrative in *Amenemhet* is concentrated on a single incident, with the result that the proverbs of which the author makes use lack variety.

8. *Theme.* The cry of King Amenemhet, 'It was he who ate my food that raised up troops against me', referring to the fact that the conspirators belonged to the king's most intimate circle, probably including some of his own sons, summarizes the main narrative theme of the book. This is also one of the main themes of the Succession Narrative, where it is applied to a number of persons: Absalom, Ahithophel, Meribbaal. In both cases the old king dies disillusioned, and it is this disillusionment which provides the occasion for the political testament.

6. Conclusion

It is not essential to the present argument to suppose that the author of the Succession Narrative was familiar with the *Instruction of Amenemhet*, the *Story of Sinuhe*, or the other Egyptian works which have been referred to, although such a supposition would not, in view of what has been said above about bilingual scribes at David's and Solomon's court, be unreasonable. Certainly no direct literary dependence can be proved, and the style of the Succession Narrative is the purest Hebrew style. Nor is it suggested that the Egyptian literary tradition was the only, or even the main, source of the author's inspiration. The Succession Narrative stands firmly in the line of development of the Israelite narrative tradition.[63] Nevertheless it is a fact that the Succession Narrative is immeasurably superior in conception, in technique and in psychological insight to any of its Hebrew predecessors, or indeed to its successors; and in other ways also—especially in its casting of proverbial literature into narrative form—it is unique in Hebrew literature. These characteristics, which indicate an extremely sudden burst of cultural maturity at the court of Solomon, require an explanation.

A great deal must be conceded—especially in view of the fact that this work had no true successors—to the individual genius of the author. This cannot in any case be denied, because his literary achievement is superior to even the best models, whether native or foreign. But such models there must have been; and in view of the fact that the author was himself a scribe at the court of Solomon, at a time when foreign, and especially Egyptian, cultural and literary influence was strong, it is impossible to regard as irrelevant the fact that Egypt had produced, at a very similar time in its own history, a sudden burst of literary activity which bears marked resemblances to that of Israel's 'enlightenment'.

The political novel, the sophisticated psychological novel, and the narrative based on wisdom themes were all known in Egypt long before the age of Solomon, and continued to be known and read for many centuries after their composition. Whether the author of the Succession Narrative knew the Egyptian literature of the twelfth Dynasty itself, or whether he was heir, more indirectly, to a literary tradition which began at that period, there

[63] On this see especially von Rad, 'Beginnings'.

is insufficient evidence to determine; but that such a literature was among his models must be regarded as extremely probable; and the comparison which has been undertaken in this chapter confirms the conclusions which have been reached about the character and aims of the Succession Narrative in the earlier chapters of this book.

INDEX OF AUTHORS

Albright, W. F., 2
Aldred, C., 105
Alt, A., 1, 4, 5, 17
Ap-Thomas, D. R., 98
Auerbach, E., 11, 17, 43

Begrich, J., 3
Bentzen, A., 48
Boer, P. A. H. de, 57
Breasted, J. H., 96
Bright, J., 54
Brunner, H., 3, 5, 74, 105, 107, 113
Buck, A. de, 110, 111, 113

Carlson, R. A., 56
Cazelles, H., 2, 81, 91
Cowley, A. E., 76

Dijk, J. J. A. van, 72
Donner, H., 3
Driver, G. R., 3
Driver, S. R., 18, 23, 45
Duesberg, H., 1, 4, 56, 79
Dürr, L., 3, 65

Eissfeldt, O., 1, 4, 8, 10, 12, 13, 25, 54
Erman, A., 71, 76, 101, 102, 103, 107, 108

Galling, K., 1, 4
Gardiner, A. H., 102, 103, 108, 110, 111
Gehman, H. S., 11, 16, 33
Gemser, B., 4, 91
Gerstenberger, E., 5
Gottwald, N. K., 2
Gressmann, H., 3f.
Griffith, F. Ll., 62
Gunkel, H., 31
Gunn, B., 110
Guthrie, H. H., 56

Hermann, A., 98, 99, 100, 101
Herrmann, S., 98, 100, 101

Hertzberg, H. W., 8. 11, 23, 34, 39, 52
Humbert, P., 4, 97

Jacob, E., 11, 16, 47, 50

Kayatz, C., 4
Kees, H., 109
Klostermann, A., 65

Lambert, W. G., 72
Lefebvre, G., 96, 98, 102, 103
Leimbach, H. A., 23
Lindblom, J., 5
Lods, A., 8, 10, 48, 50
Luther, B., 10, 12, 16, 17, 19, 43, 46, 50

Malfroy, J., 5
McKane, W., 11, 43, 48, 62, 67
McKenzie, J. L., 1, 4, 7, 81
Meyer, E., 10, 50
Montgomery, J. A., 11, 16, 33
Morenz, S., 96, 97

North, C. R., 18, 47
Noth, M., 3, 4, 5, 8, 30, 51, 56, 78, 98, 100

Otto, E., 100, 110, 111

Peet, T. E., 102, 103, 104
Pfeiffer, R. H., 10, 47, 62
Plumley, J. M., 62
Posener, G., 103, 105, 106, 107, 108, 110, 111, 112, 113

Rad, G. von, 1, 3, 4, 5, 6, 7, 8, 10, 11, 19, 25, 35, 43, 46, 50, 56, 61, 63, 64, 66, 69, 76, 77, 78, 83, 98, 115
Roeder, G., 102, 103, 105
Rost, L., 8, 10, 12, 16, 19, 20, 21, 23, 35, 39, 45, 46, 51, 53, 54, 66, 69

Scott, R. B. Y., 1, 5, 70
Smith, M., 11, 16, 50
Spiegel, J., 103, 104
Spuler, B., 5
Suys, E., 103, 105

Thomas, D. W., 2, 62

Vandier, J., 112
Vaux, R. de, 3, 98, 100
Vriezen, T. C., 53, 54

Weill, R., 97
Weinfeld, M., 5
Weir, C. J. Mullo, 2
Weiser, A., 11, 18, 52
Wellhausen, J., 10, 11, 16
Whybray, R. N., 4, 70, 73, 74, 75
Wilson, J., A. 62, 76
Würthwein, E., 1

Zimmerli, W., 73